RELUCTANT
ENTERTAINER'S
BIG BOARDS
AND MORE

RELUCTANT ENTERTAINER'S BIG BOARDS AND MORE

100 Mix-and-Match
Recipes to Make Any
Gathering Great

SANDY COUGHLIN

FAIR WINDS

Inspiring | Educating | Creating | Entertaining

Brimming with creative inspiration, how-to projects, and useful information to enrich your everyday life, quarto.com is a favorite destination for those pursuing their interests and passions.

First Published in 2022 by Fair Winds Press, an imprint of The Quarto Group,
100 Cummings Center, Suite 265-D, Beverly, MA 01915, USA.
T (978) 282-9590 F (978) 283-2742 Quarto.com

Fair Winds Press titles are also available at discount for retail, wholesale, promotional, and bulk purchase. For details, contact the Special Sales Manager by email at specialsales@quarto.com or by mail at The Quarto Group, Attn: Special Sales Manager, 100 Cummings Center, Suite 265-D, Beverly, MA 01915, USA.

26 25 24 23 22   1 2 3 4 5

ISBN: 978-0-7603-7807-6

Digital edition published in 2022

eISBN: 978-0-7603-7808-3

Library of Congress Cataloging-in-Publication Data
Names: Coughlin, Sandy, author.
Title: Reluctant entertainer's big boards and more : 100 mix-and-match recipes to make any gathering great / Sandy Coughlin.
Description: Beverley, MA : Fair Winds, 2022. | Includes index. | Summary: "In this fun, flexible cookbook, charcuterie board guru Sandy Coughlin (@reluctantentertainer) offers 100 recipes for both indoors and out that make hosting any size event, anywhere, a breeze. As the original Big Board influencer, Sandy Coughlin reimagined the charcuterie board as a stunning surface for family gatherings, holiday spreads, delicious desserts, and more. Now, she expands her repertoire with individual recipes for any occasion, large or small. Arranged by season, and including gluten-free, dairy-free, and plant-based options for customizable convenience, The Reluctant Entertainer's Big Boards and More will spark your culinary imagination with the endless possibilities of boards. Elements include: International inspiration for the curious cook: Regional recipes from around the world to light your travel fuse Just close friends: Smaller boards for 2-4 people, whether it's date night or game night Special days and seasonal celebrations: For weddings, holidays, or just a birthday bash The great outdoors: Portable, sustainable recipes for camping, road trips, and outdoor entertaining Whether you're a board enthusiast already or a first-time host, The Reluctant Entertainer's Big Boards and More has everything you need to make a serious splash-all year round"-- Provided by publisher.
Identifiers: LCCN 2022022603 | ISBN 9780760378076 (board) | ISBN 9780760378083 (ebook)
Subjects: LCSH: Seasonal cooking. | Entertaining. | LCGFT: Cookbooks.
Classification: LCC TX714 .C6974 2022 | DDC 641.5/64--dc23/eng/20220524
LC record available at https://lccn.loc.gov/2022022603

Design: Laura Klynstra
Photography: Abby Coughlin

Printed in China
Printed in USA

To Abigail Ellen Rose, my lovely, talented daughter. For your photography, love of cooking and the great outdoors, food styling, and so much more. Your test kitchen is one of the greatest places Dad and I love to linger in. Your gentle and strong spirit infuses this book.

To all my outdoor enthusiasts and fellow board-lovers—this book is for you. Get outside, try something new, bring a board and some food, and invite your friends to create new, lasting memories.

CONTENTS

INTRODUCTION

Home is the center of our lives, the ground beneath our feet, the place that shelters and sustains us. The center of a home is always the kitchen; a hearth and heartbeat that radiates warmth and comfort.

I am fortunate enough to have fond memories of growing up in a very happy home. Looking back, I can see how many of those memories are linked to food.

I remember devouring peanut butter and jelly sandwiches while struggling over homework, nabbing homemade cookies from the cookie jar when I was sure my parents were asleep, and making my first loaf of bread that didn't turn out (does it ever?), my sisters laughing at the dab of flour that ended up on the tip of my nose.

Back then, home was the place where I was nourished and cherished, so much more than a roof, walls, and appliances in classic avocado green.

So, naturally, that's what I want my home to be now, for my family, friends, and guests—a place of safety, sustenance, and simple joys, a place to build connections and memories that last. Don't we all?

That's exactly why I wrote this book. Because deep in our souls, we instinctively understand that homemade food and love are linked. Whether you're looking to recreate a home you once loved, or start a new one, my Big Board is a great place to start.

It's the love and hospitality of food that excites me and my daughter, Abby, who took the beautiful pictures in this book and helped create many of the recipes. It's why I launched my Big Board in 2020, and created our first board cookbook, *Big Boards for Families,* in the same year. And it's why we made this book, *Reluctant Entertainer's Big Boards and More,* for you.

We hope it inspires you to make your house a home and your neighborhood a community. Put the recipes in this book to work and you'll be well on your way to achieving this because nothing brings people together faster than the promise of a delicious meal.

Because we feast with our eyes as well as our mouths, we hope you'll find joy and beauty in Abby's photography, and that it will tempt you to make these recipes your own.

More than anything else, we hope this book will help you make every day, occasion, and location—whether it be the kitchen counter, your formal dining room, or the great outdoors—a place that feels like home.

HOW THE BIG BOARD WAS BORN

When we launched our line of Big Boards, with their all-important lip, clever undercut handles, and food-safe surfaces, in the middle of a worldwide pandemic, we had no inkling of what the response would be.

Happily, it was wildly enthusiastic! So much so that keeping up with demand was a challenge, but one we were thrilled to accept. At our customers' request, we quickly added different sizes, shapes, and shades to the original Big Board collection.

Now, we're excited to announce the latest addition to the Big Board Family. Except it's not really big. In fact, it's kind of small. It's also kind of genius.

Our new Travel Board sports a smart double hinge and raised lip, with a rustic leather strap, our iconic handles, and food-safe surface. It's perfect for the outdoors, smaller spaces, and smaller needs—great for serving up to four on the go.

When we launched the Big Board during a difficult time, so many people reached out to tell me that it made their holiday season even cozier and extra special. They sent photos of lovingly prepared boards with an abundance of delicious spreads and happy faces—messages I'll always cherish. Now that the Board has become part of their lives, I hope they'll embrace the opportunity to use it again and again, for occasions big and small.

BOARDS FOR EVERY SEASON AND REGION

We divided this book into seasons to give you year-round inspiration and the chance to make every gathering, from holidays to plain old weekdays, a little more joyful.

We love to travel but, like so many others, we've had our wings clipped a bit in recent years. We're really looking forward to hitting the road again soon, and we know we're not alone. With that in mind, we've added some travel-inspired board recipes from diverse regions of the world, drawn from both our own travels and our vacation dreams. While these recipes aren't authentic by any means, we hope that they feed your imagination, perhaps inspiring you to explore and welcome other cultures and cuisines into your kitchen and home.

And though big gatherings are perfect for our biggest Big Boards, we know that not everyone likes to have over enough people to field a football team. With that in mind, we've included small-portion recipes for smaller board spreads. If you love the recipe but do need to feed a crowd, simply halve it for a dinner party.

One of my favorite things about this cookbook is its flexibility. We've made it easy to create your own boards with the recipes that you like by giving ideas how to mix and match. There's no wrong way to create a board. They are like art: Make what your heart tells you!

And finally, our outdoor board ideas will help you get to know your neighbors and explore new ways to get outside—with a delicious meal or snack ready to go on our handy new Travel Board.

KITCHEN ESSENTIALS

I use the same bowls and tongs over and over. It's actually quite simple and fun to focus on the food and not worry as much about the accessories. This is what I keep on hand:

- Hot pads (essential if you are serving something hot, as you do not want to scorch your board) or trivets
- Small- and medium-size tongs
- Salad servers and serving spoons
- Knives and spreaders
- A variety of bowls between 2 and 6 inches (5 and 15 cm) wide for sauces, dips, and condiments (a nesting bowl set is well worth the investment because it offers many sizes)
- Use what you already have for dinner plates, platters, baking pans, casserole dishes, or pots.

FIND YOUR INSPIRATION

Think about your table spread the way an artist approaches a blank canvas. Consider what will be the focal point, as well as colors that pop in the right places.

Serve a favorite family recipe and talk about what it means to you. Talk about the history of the recipe and why it's so important to you.

Look to the changing seasons, inspired by colors, tastes, and seasonal foods, which are often found at your local farmers' market.

Let special events be a guide—think bridal and baby showers, tailgating, picnicking, camping, backyard barbecues, pool parties, birthdays, achievement celebrations, holidays, and more.

Explore different parts of the world and their culinary traditions. Read a book or watch a show about a given country while feasting on its cuisine. Not only will you discover new ingredients and dishes, but you'll better understand food's connection to culture.

For multigenerational gatherings, invite grandparents, aunts and uncles, or elderly neighbors over to enjoy a board.

You're inspired by the idea of boards, but not the cooking process? That's okay, because with boards you can find almost everything in your local deli, bakery, or farmers' market.

SIMPLE STEPS TO MAKING YOUR CREATION

1. Plan your menu by writing down the recipes or taking a picture of the ones in this book.

2. Search your pantry before you go shopping. You might already have some of the ingredients, or substitute with something similar, saving your family money and time.

3. Know how many people you are serving; scale the size of the board to the number you are feeding.

4. Decide which ingredients or main dish will be the star.

5. When you're tight for time, take shortcuts. Buy a rotisserie chicken, brownies at the bakery, or potato salad at the deli. Not everything needs to be from scratch.

6. If guests are coming over, ask them to bring an aspect, or wedge, for the board. You might think this is a burden, but it's not. Good guests want to contribute.

7. Prep as much as you can in advance. For example, you can make the main dish ahead of time and assemble the board about 1 hour before serving.

OTHER WAYS TO USE THE BOARDS

There are so many options to store the Big Boards! My favorite is in the center of the dining table. For our big square table, the ebonized 12 x 36 inch (30 x 76 cm) board fits perfectly, with a giant candle, a plant, and a stack of napkins. Or use it on a sideboard to hold candles, flowers, or family photos. So many options!

We love our maple rectangle board in our master bathroom as a tub caddy. Think candles, books, fragrant soap, or herbal-scented sugar scrub. They're also perfect for holding a cup of tea or glass of wine while you enjoy a nice long soak.

One of our readers sent us a gorgeous photo of the long board she took to a wedding where all the guests signed the board. How special is that? No matter the setting, you're sure to find a use for these boards beyond serving a belly-filling meal.

PART 1

SPRING/ SUMMER

"Live in the sunshine, swim the sea, drink the wild air."
—Ralph Waldo Emerson

I'd add . . . *gather and eat with the ones you love!*

For many of us, spring and summer are the best time of the year. It's when we get outdoors and reconnect with the sun, whether it's a day at the beach, a beautiful hike, or just a simple picnic.

It's when babies are born in our pastures and fields, and flowers gently push through the warmer soil and captivate our senses. It's the time to update our table linens, showcase those flowers, and serve up some of the delicious boards in this section.

It's also when we reconnect with neighbors—sometimes on the spur of a moment—after a long, cold winter. My parents were great at last-minute visits. Long chats over the fence often led to a dinner invitation. Dad would carefully take his axe to the ice blocks my mom made from used, paper milk cartons. They used this ice to make the best homemade vanilla ice cream ever. I still remember Mom handing me the white paddle to lick, dripping with her special recipe.

Maybe you can't buy happiness, but you can sure buy (or make!) ice cream.

So, let's unplug from our phones, turn off Netflix, and get outside. Bring your board with you, complete with a great meal, something sweet, and a really good bottle of wine.

CHAPTER 1

Keeping it Small: Recipes for 2 to 4

Cucumber Spicy Feta Dip

Although I'm calling this a "dip," it can be much more than that! I like to use this recipe as a dressing for sautéed veggies, a spread on flatbreads and sandwiches, and even melted over scrambled eggs. Sautéing the shallots and garlic mellows their sharpness and adds a sweetness that balances the heat of the serrano chili. If you're sensitive to heat, make sure to seed the chili and/or halve the amount. If you want to omit the chili altogether, replace it with a quarter of a seeded green bell pepper. Additionally, if you don't have chives, you can substitute them with green onion.

Makes 1¾ cups (300 g) | Prep time: 10 minutes, plus 5 minutes chill time | Cook time: 5 minutes

2 Persian cucumbers, grated

3 tablespoons (45 ml) olive oil, divided

1 medium shallot, minced

1 large clove garlic, minced

1 teaspoon fresh ground black pepper

1 teaspoon salt, plus more to taste

⅓ cup (77 g) Greek yogurt

⅓ cup (75 g) fresh feta, crumbled and divided

1 tablespoon (3 g) chives, roughly chopped

1 serrano chili, seeded, roughly chopped (substitute jalapeño or ¼ green bell pepper)

1½ teaspoons pomegranate molasses (optional)

1 teaspoon honey

mint, julienned

1. Add the grated cucumber to a fine-mesh sieve and season with a pinch of salt. Set aside to drain.

2. In a small skillet over medium-high heat, add 2 tablespoons (30 ml) olive oil; once hot, add the shallot, garlic, pepper, and a pinch of salt. Sauté 5 minutes until softened. Transfer to a bowl and refrigerate for 5 minutes to cool.

3. Add the cooled shallot mixture to a food processor, along with the Greek yogurt, ¼ cup (37.5 g) feta, chives, serrano chili, pomegranate molasses, honey, and salt. Purée until thick and mostly smooth, about 2 minutes. Using your hands, squeeze the excess water from the cucumbers, then transfer to the dip and fold in, along with the remaining feta.

4. Garnish with the remaining olive oil and mint. Serve cold with crackers, warm flatbread, and fresh vegetables.

Baba Ghanoush with Poblano Chilis

Baba ghanoush, a recipe with Arabic roots and many different variations throughout the Middle East, is a thick, creamy, smokey dip with bright lemon flavors. It contrasts wonderfully with the crunchy, funky Seedy Kimchi Crackers, and, if served with the Mediterranean-inspired Cucumber Spicy Feta Dip, provides your mouth a cool, buttery escape from the fiery serrano chili. Poblano chili is not an original ingredient in baba ghanoush, of course, but its charred, grassy flavor blends perfectly.

Makes 2 cups (450 g) | Prep time: 65–70 minutes

2 eggplants

2–3 large poblano chiles

¼ cup (60 g) tahini

1 medium lemon, zested

1½ tablespoons (22.5 ml) lemon juice (about ½ lemon)

½ teaspoon kosher salt, plus more to taste

FOR THE BOARD

cucumber

tomatoes

red bell pepper

olives

warmed pita

carrots

celery

radish

1 recipe Seedy Kimchi Crackers

½ recipe Baba Ghanoush

NOTE

- The process of charring the eggplant takes about 45 minutes, and unfortunately, it can't be rushed, because it will dry out. Additionally, the longer the eggplant sits, the better the smokey flavor.

1. Using a fork, prick the skin of the eggplant to prevent unwanted explosions! Place the eggplant on the grates of a gas range stove over a medium-low flame, or on a cast-iron grill on the stovetop or grill. Turn every 15 minutes or so, about 45 minutes total depending on the size of the eggplant, until the skin is fully charred, cracked, and beginning to release liquid. Put into a colander to drain excess liquid; about 15 minutes. Once drained, peel off the skin and remove the stem. To maintain texture, use a fork or your fingers to separate it into stringy pieces. (Preparing the eggplant can be done the day before making the chili, if needed—just cover and store in the refrigerator until ready to use.)

2. While the eggplant chars, char the poblanos on a baking sheet, under a broiler set to high. Blister and blacken the skin, 6–8 minutes per side—this can also be done over an open flame. Once the skins have blackened, place into a container or wrap in plastic to steam, about 5 minutes. Once steamed and cooled, peel off skin and remove seeds. Roughly chop and set aside.

3. In a medium mixing bowl, using a fork, combine the eggplant, poblano, tahini, lemon zest, lemon juice, and salt. If you'd like a smoother consistency, pulse in a food processor about 10 times. Refrigerate until ready to serve.

Seedy Kimchi Crackers

Serves 4–6 | Prep time: 5 minutes | Cook time: 45–55 minutes

¼ cup (40 g) raw pumpkin seeds

¼ cup (42 g) whole flaxseeds

⅛ cup (22 g) chia seeds

¼ cup (36 g) raw sesame seeds

3 tablespoons (24 g) black sesame seeds (substitute white)

¼ cup (48 g) raw sunflower seeds

2 teaspoons ground flaxseed

½ cup (63 g) corn flour

1 teaspoon fresh ground black pepper

1 teaspoon salt, plus more to taste

2 teaspoons nutritional yeast (optional)

¼ cup (59 ml) neutral oil

⅓ cup (80 ml) kimchi brine (substitute with a salty pickle brine or just water)

⅔ cup (160 ml) water

1. Preheat the oven to 350°F (180°C, or gas mark 4). Line a baking sheet with parchment.

2. Stir together all the seeds, corn flour, pepper, salt, nutritional yeast, and oil in a bowl. Bring the kimchi or pickle brine and the water to a boil, then pour over the seeds and stir until thickened. Add salt to taste. Using a greased spatula, spread the dough into a single thin layer, about ¼" (6 mm) thick.

3. Bake for 45–55 minutes until crisp, slightly darkened in color, and fragrant. Let cool completely before breaking into large pieces and enjoying with dips.

Pictured page 18.

Corn Bacon and Cheddar Waffles

When my kids were growing up, they loved waffles even more than pancakes—mostly because the wells could hold a generous amount of maple syrup. While regular flour waffles are delicious, waffles made with cornmeal, bacon, and cheese are next level. The cornmeal and fillings give the final product a toothsome, chewy, crisp texture that holds up sturdily even with copious amounts of syrup drizzled on top. The final texture may vary a little depending on the type of waffle maker you have, but no matter what, the flavor will be delicious.

Great for an indulgent breakfast sandwich, too!

Serves 2–4 | Prep time: 10 minutes | Cook time: 10–15 minutes

WAFFLES

½ cup (62.5 g) all-purpose flour

¾ cup (94.5 g) corn flour (finely ground cornmeal)

½ teaspoon baking soda

¾ teaspoon baking powder

¾ teaspoon salt

2 teaspoons white sugar

¾ cup (175 ml) buttermilk

1 egg

2½ tablespoons (35 g) butter, melted and cooled

1 cup (120 g) sharp cheddar cheese

¾ cup (60 g) chopped cooked bacon

SERVE WITH

eggs and maple syrup

1. In a medium mixing bowl, combine the flour, corn flour, baking soda, baking powder, salt, and sugar. In a separate small bowl, whisk together the buttermilk, egg, and butter. Mix the wet ingredients into the dry until just combined, then fold in the cheddar cheese and bacon.

2. Cook the waffles until crisp—the time will depend on your waffle maker, so follow the manufacturer's instructions.

3. Keep the waffles warm and crispy in the oven, set to 170°F (77°C), as you cook the eggs and warm the syrup.

Sweet Soy Marinated Salmon with Cold Lemongrass Soba Noodles

When the weather is warm, I typically want to eat refreshing, light meals. Cold soba noodles are perfect for satiating my pasta cravings in the summertime. There are a few reasons why this noodle dish is best served chilled. First, the peppery ginger and citric lemongrass are enhanced in the refrigerator. Second, chilling allows you to prepare it ahead of time and serve it straight from the refrigerator; all you need to do is spruce it up with some garnishes. However, this dish can be served warm as well if you just skip the instructions to chill the ingredients.

Serves 4 | Prep time: 15 minutes, plus 20 minutes marinating time | Cook time: 30 minutes

FOR THE SALMON AND MARINADE

¼ cup (60 ml) soy sauce

2 teaspoons dark soy sauce (substitute 4 teaspoons [20 ml] regular soy sauce)

¼ cup (60 ml) mirin (rice cooking wine)

4 teaspoons (16 g) Dijon mustard

1 tablespoon (8 g) ginger, grated

2–3 tablespoons lemongrass (about 3–4 stalks), bruised and minced (see recipe note)

¼ cup (85 g) brown sugar or honey

½ (120 ml) and 1/3 cup (80 ml) water

⅓ cup (48 g) toasted sesame seeds, coarsely ground, divided

1 shallot, minced

4 x 6–8 oz (170–225 g) salmon filets (24–32 oz [680.4 g–1 kg] total)

MAKE THE MARINADE

1. In a medium mixing bowl, combine the soy sauce, dark soy sauce, mirin, Dijon mustard, ginger, lemongrass, brown sugar, ½ cup (120 ml) water, and 3 tablespoons (24 g) sesame seeds.

2. Pour about ½ cup (120 ml) of the marinade over the salmon filets. Toss to coat, press the air out of the bag, and marinate for 20 minutes.

COOK THE SALMON

3. Heat a nonstick skillet over medium-high heat with 1 teaspoon of neutral oil. Add the salmon, skin side down, and the remaining marinade from the bag to the pan. Reduce the heat to medium and baste the salmon with the marinade until mostly cooked through, about 6–8 minutes, then flip and cook an additional 4–5 minutes. Use a fork to flake the salmon apart into large pieces, discarding the skin, and place in a wide bowl. Refrigerate for 10–15 minutes to cool down.

4. When all the ingredients have cooled, toss the noodles in the sauce, then add the flaked salmon, remaining toasted sesame seeds, snow peas, green onion, red chili, and the cucumber. Toss and garnish with a few pinches of micro greens. Return the salad to the refrigerator to chill for an additional 2 hours, if desired.

FOR THE NOODLES

½–¾ lb. (225–340 g) soba noodles

2 teaspoons toasted sesame oil, substitute neutral oil

1 teaspoon neutral oil

¾ cup (74 g) snow peas, julienned

¼ cup (26 g) green onion, thinly sliced

1 Fresno red chili, finely diced

2 Persian cucumbers, seeds removed, finely diced

micro greens to garnish

5. While the salmon marinates, reduce the sauce. In a small skillet, add the remaining marinade, the shallots, and 1/3 cup (80 ml) more water; bring to a simmer over medium-high heat. Reduce the heat to medium-low and simmer until thickened, about 12–15 minutes. Remove from the heat, transfer to a bowl, and refrigerate until cold.

6. Prepare the noodles according to the package directions, making sure to cook al dente. Once cooked, rinse very well with cold water to remove the starch. Drain, toss to coat in the toasted sesame oil, and refrigerate.

NOTES

- To bruise the lemongrass, remove the greenest top part, leaving the bottom 3–4 inches (7.5–10 cm), and the first few fibrous layers. Next, use a rolling pin, a pestle, or a meat mallet to press down on the thick, white end of the stalk—this releases its oils, which lends more flavor to the dish. The lemongrass will be noticeably fragrant after doing this.

- You can substitute half of a large English cucumber for the Persian cucumber, just make sure it is seeded. To do this, cut the cucumber in half and run a spoon down the center to scoop out the watery, seedy interior.

- To grind the sesame seeds, use a mortar and pestle until coarsely ground.

Grilled Caesar Salad with Homemade Caesar Dressing

Caesar salads can be hit or miss—sometimes they're perfectly balanced with acid, umami, salt, and peppery heat, other times they taste like romaine drenched in lemony mayonnaise. It is no secret that a good Caesar salad has Parmesan cheese—but the *real* secret is the savory anchovy flavor. Don't shy away from the fish sauce because of its (delicious) potency; in a well-made dressing, the flavors will sing in harmony. This Caesar dressing takes inspiration from Japan, with the use of an egg yolk and vinegar-based mayonnaise (similar to Japan's Kewpie mayonnaise), the Southeast Asian influence of fish sauce rather than Worcestershire sauce, and the addition of white pepper. (You can, of course use a store-bought dressing if you're short on time.)

Serves 2 | Prep time: 10 minutes, plus 5–20 minutes to make the dressing | Cook time: 5 minutes

FOR THE UNSALTED MAYONNAISE BASE

3 egg yolks

1½ tablespoons (25 ml) apple cider vinegar, plus more to taste

¾ cup (177 ml) neutral oil

FOR THE DRESSING

½ teaspoon black pepper

¼ teaspoon white pepper

1 tablespoon (15 ml) fish sauce

1 tablespoon (15 ml) and 2 teaspoons lemon juice

1 teaspoon lemon zest

2 cloves garlic, grated

½ teaspoon salt, plus more to taste

¼ cup (25 g) crumbled Parmesan, plus 2 tablespoons (10 g) to garnish

MAKE THE MAYONNAISE

1. In a narrow, tall cup—preferably the one that comes with immersion blenders—add the egg yolks, vinegar, and oil. Press and keep the blender flat against the bottom of the cup for 30 seconds as you blend on high, until thickened, pale, and emulsified. The consistency will be looser and thinner than store-bought mayonnaise.

2. To the mayonnaise, add the black pepper, white pepper, fish sauce, lemon juice and zest, garlic, and salt. Blend on high until smooth, moving the blender up and down as needed. Once combined, fold in the Parmesan; taste and adjust for additional fish sauce and vinegar. Refrigerate until ready to use.

3. To make the dressing by hand, cradle the bowl in a wet towel—this keeps it stuck in place as you whisk. Add the egg yolks and vinegar to the bowl and whisk to combine. Next, stream in the oil, slowly and a little at a time, whisking constantly. Whisk until all of the oil is added and the mayonnaise is thick and pale in color. Whisk in the black pepper, white pepper, fish sauce, lemon juice and zest, garlic, and salt until smooth. Finally, fold in the Parmesan cheese. If you're using premade mayonnaise, whisk in the spices, fish sauce, lemon juice, zest, garlic, and Parmesan; taste for additional vinegar and salt and refrigerate.

(continued)

FOR THE SALAD

10 cherry tomatoes

⅓ cup (80 ml) olive oil

2 large romaine hearts, wilted leaves removed and halved lengthwise with base intact to hold leaves together

½ small Italian baguette, sliced lengthwise

salt and pepper to season

ASSEMBLE THE SALAD

4. Spear five tomatoes onto two small, soaked, wooden skewers. Preheat a grill—or, if making indoors, a large cast-iron skillet—over medium-high heat. Brush a generous amount of olive oil onto the cut side of the romaine hearts, avoid stacking cherry tomatoes. Season the lettuce, bread, and tomatoes with salt and pepper. When the grill is sufficiently hot, place the lettuce, bread, and tomatoes onto the grates until lightly charred and browned, 60–90 seconds for the lettuce, 1–2 minutes for the bread, and 1–2 minutes per side for the cherry tomatoes.

5. Remove from the grill and plate; drizzle with dressing and garnish with crumbled Parmesan.

NOTES

- The dressing calls for you to make your own, unsalted, mayonnaise base, one that can also be used as a spread, added to dips, or in other dressings—just add salt to taste. If you want to skip making the mayonnaise altogether, use ¾ cup (175 g) of Kewpie mayo or regular mayonnaise; the flavors will be slightly different, but still delicious.

- Makes about 1 scant cup (225 g) of mayonnaise.

- I recommend using a high-quality fish sauce like Red Boat when making anything with fish sauce.

- If you have trouble emulsifying the egg yolks and find the final product too runny, simply whisk in a spoonful of mayonnaise to help the dressing come together

- For the garlic, grate on a microplane or use a mortar and pestle and a pinch of coarse salt to crush into a paste.

- Adjust the amount of lettuce and bread, depending on how many people you're feeding.

- To add protein, the shrimp for the Grilled Shrimp Cocktail Skewers on page 97 would be *so delicious here!*

Spicy and Sweet Melon Mint Feta Salad

Simple salads are a must during hot summer months. This sweet and spicy side dish is both refreshingly cool—with melon, mint, and cucumber—and fiery hot from jalapeño peppers. Feta cheese provides some relief from the heat, and pairs perfectly with the sweetness of floral honey and tangy chili-lime salt. If your spice tolerance is low, swap in green bell pepper to achieve the grassy, fresh flavor of jalapeño. Additionally, jicama is a great substitute for any of the vegetables and fruits, as it provides crunch and takes on other flavors well. If you don't have time to cut the ingredients into cubes, simply skip it and chop it into bite-size pieces.

Serves 4 | Prep time: 5 minutes

2–3 cups cantaloupe, cut into 1¼–1½" (2.6–3.5 cm) cubes

2–3 cups watermelon, cut into 1¼–1½" (2.6–3.5 cm) cubes

2 large Persian cucumbers, cut into 1¼–1½" (2.6–3.5 cm) cubes

8 oz (225 g) feta cheese, cut into 1¼–1½" (2.6–3.5 cm) cubes

2 jalapeños, cut into ½" (1 cm) half moons

honey to drizzle

3 tablespoons (18 g) fresh-chopped mint, plus 10 small whole leaves

3 teaspoons (18 g) Tajin chili-lime seasoning salt

1. On a large platter or plate, arrange a wide, single layer of cantaloupe, watermelon, cucumber, feta, and jalapeño, drizzle with honey and a sprinkle of seasoning. Repeat two more times, and finish with honey, mint, and a generous dusting of Tajin. Serve chilled.

Herby Fingerling Potato Salad with Crispy Fried Shallots

Inspired by the classic potato salad, this is a starch with a lighter, fresher spin. The dressing is creamy, but tastes similar to a sweet vinaigrette, with the punchy flavor of green onion and herbaceous, citrusy notes from the dill. When boiling the potatoes, make sure the water is salty for a well-seasoned result. While the fried shallots aren't required, they do add a crunchy sweetness.

Serves 4–6 | Prep time: 10 minutes | Cook time: 30 minutes, plus 20 minutes cooling time

1½ lb. (680 g) fingerling potatoes

2–3 tablespoons (36–54 g) salt, to season water

1 tablespoon (14 g) mayonnaise

1 tablespoon (15 ml) rice vinegar

¾ teaspoon apple cider vinegar

¼ cup (16 g) dill, minced, plus more to garnish

¼ cup (26 g) green onions, minced

1½ teaspoons Dijon mustard

1 teaspoon ground black pepper

1½ teaspoons honey

2 tablespoons (30 g) sour cream

1 cup (240 g) Crispy Fried Shallots recipe opposite (if you don't have time to make, use store-bought fried onions)

1. In a medium saucepan, add the potatoes, and fill with water until the potatoes are covered; season the water very generously with salt, 2–3 tablespoons (36–54 g). Bring the water to a boil over a high heat, then reduce to medium and simmer. Cook the potatoes until they can easily be pierced with a fork all the way through; remove the small potatoes if they finish cooking before the large. The cook time will depend on the size of your potatoes but should be 25–30 minutes. Drain the potatoes and let cool in a single layer for approximately 20 minutes.

2. While the potatoes cook, combine the mayonnaise, rice vinegar, apple cider vinegar, dill, green onion, Dijon, pepper, honey, and sour cream; whisk until smooth, taste for salt, and refrigerate until ready to use.

3. Cut the potatoes into large pieces and transfer to a medium mixing bowl, along with the dressing. Toss to coat. Garnish with the crispy fried shallots and additional dill and mint.

NOTES

- For the crispy fried shallots, the amount of oil will vary depending on the size of your sauce pot; it will likely be around 1½–2 cups (355–475 ml) of oil.

- Have a paper towel-lined plate and a colander over a bowl ready to immediately drain the shallots.

- Save the remaining oil. It's delicious and can be used to sauté or fry vegetables, to make eggs, or in salad dressing.

Crispy Fried Shallots

Makes about 1 cup (240 g) | Prep time: 5 minutes | Cook time: 28 minutes

4 large shallots, sliced ¼" (6 mm) thick

neutral oil (canola, vegetable, grapeseed)

salt to season

1. In a cold, small sauce pot, add the shallots. Pour in enough oil to cover them. Bring the heat to medium-high; once the shallots begin to bubble and fry, reduce the heat to medium-low and fry for 20–25 minutes. Stir frequently and keep an eye on them toward the end. When the shallots turn an amber color and become fragrant, immediately drain in the colander, transfer to the paper towel-lined plate, and season with salt. As they cool, they will crisp and darken in color slightly. Set aside until ready to garnish the potatoes.

Oven-roasted Caramelized Onions and Chicken Thighs

This recipe was born from my dislike for nursing caramelized onions on the stovetop for 1 hour, fearing that if I left them unattended for a minute, they would scorch. Happily, I discovered that roasting them in the oven in rendered chicken fat, at a high temperature, yielded the same flavors and texture. While the onions do need to be stirred a few times while roasting, and there are a few temperature changes to pay attention to, it's still infinitely easier than standing at the stove forever. I do add a bit of sugar to help with caramelization and flavor; adjust the amount to your liking. Additionally, bone-in, skin-on chicken thighs are great for roasting, because their fat content allows them to endure the oven without drying out. To serve on a board, enjoy the chicken and onions with crunchy bread, roasted vegetables, and a garden salad.

Makes 2½ cups (800 g) caramelized onions and 4–5 chicken thighs | Serves 2–4 | Prep time: 10 minutes, plus 30 minutes to 48 minutes for chicken to rest at room temperature | Cook time: 2 hours 45 minutes

4–5 bone-in, skin-on chicken thighs

salt and pepper to season

1 tablespoon (15 ml) oil, olive or neutral

2 tablespoons (28 ml) butter

3 large yellow onions sliced into ¼"
(6 mm) half moons

1½ tablespoons (19.5 g) white sugar or
(10.1 g) honey

3 cups (710 ml) white wine

4 sprigs thyme or rosemary

1 tablespoon (15 ml) sherry (optional),
plus more to taste

1. Preheat the oven to 425°F (220°C, or gas mark 7).

2. Season the chicken thighs with salt and pepper; 30 minutes to 48 hours in advance, gently season under the skin. Allow at least 30 minutes for the meat to rest at room temperature before searing.

3. In a shallow braising dish or oven-safe skillet with a lid, add the oil and chicken thighs, skin side down. Bring the heat to medium and allow the thighs to slowly render their fat and crisp up. Once the skin is golden and crispy, about 10 minutes, remove from the dish and set aside, leaving the rendered fat in the pan, about 4 tablespoons (60 ml).

4. In the same pan, melt the butter and add the onions; season with salt and sugar or honey and toss in the butter. Turn off the heat and add 1½ cups (355 ml) of white wine and the herbs. Roast on the center rack of the oven with the lid on for 45 minutes; stir every 20–30 minutes to ensure the edges don't burn. If your lid does not fit snuggly, add a layer of foil underneath to seal the moisture in.

5. After 45 minutes, stir in an additional 1 cup (235 ml) of wine, and increase the heat to 450°F (230°C, or gas mark 8). Roast with the lid on for 30 minutes more; then uncover and roast for 15 minutes. Toward the end

NOTES

- To make these onions without the chicken, simply add 2 more tablespoons (28 g) of butter and 2 more tablespoons (30 ml) olive oil to the braising dish before roasting.

- If the onions are looking a bit dry when you check on them, add a few splashes of wine, stock, or water every now and then.

of roasting, you may need to stir a few splashes of wine or water into the onions to make sure they don't burn.

6. Once darkened in color, softened, and fragrant, taste for salt, and stir in ½ cup (120 ml) more wine and the sherry. Reduce the heat to 400°F (200°C, or gas mark 6) and nestle the chicken thighs into the onions, skin side up. Return to the oven, with the lid off, for 30–40 more minutes, until the onions are browned around the edges and the meat reaches 165°F (75°C).

7. If the onions still need a little more time, simply remove the thighs and finish reducing on the stovetop for 10–15 minutes.

Tamarind and Lemongrass Milk-braised Pork

The origins of milk-braised pork can be found in Italian cuisine. I adapted this cooking method by pairing it with the Southeast Asian flavors of lemongrass, tamarind, and shallots. The result is an aromatic, creamy sauce, and pork that melts in your mouth. All this dish needs is a side of white rice; however, you can shake up a meal by adding it to tacos, burritos, sandwiches, and more. This pork turns out best when you season it 3 days before cooking.

Serves 2–4 | Prep time: 3 hours and 15 minutes | Cook time: 2½–3 hours

2.5–3 lb. (1.1–1.4 kg) pork shoulder, cut into 6 large pieces, fat cap removed (excess fat)

salt to season

1 tablespoon (15 ml) neutral oil (canola, vegetable, avocado)

1 large stalk lemongrass (about 3–4 tablespoons [12.6–16.8 g]), outer layers removed, minced

1½ tablespoons (9 g) ginger, minced

3–4 large shallots, quartered

¼ cup (60 g) plus 2 tablespoons (30 g) tamarind paste (unsweetened)

3½ tablespoons (70 g) honey

3 tablespoons (45 ml) fish sauce

1 tablespoon (15 ml) dark soy sauce

1¼ cups (285 ml) whole milk

1. At least 2 hours before cooking, season the pork with salt on every side and refrigerate for 1 hour. Before searing, let the meat sit out for 1 hour.

2. Preheat the oven to 325°F (170°C, or gas mark 3).

3. In the braising dish, add the neutral oil over medium-high heat. Once shimmery and hot, add the pork pieces in a single layer and brown, 3–4 minutes per side. Remove from the pan and lower the heat to medium. Add the lemongrass, ginger, and shallots and cook for 5 minutes, then add the tamarind paste, honey, fish sauce, and soy sauce. Cook 3–4 minutes, then add the milk and a generous pinch of salt. Add the browned pork back to the dish and cover.

4. Bake for 2½–3 hours until fork-tender. Skim off most of the excess fat before shredding and serving hot with rice and veggies.

NOTES

- Read how to bruise lemongrass (Lemongrass Soba Noodles on page 26).
- Use a shallow braising dish to ensure the moisture condenses on the top, and drips back onto the meat to baste it, instead of evaporating—the moisture will evaporate if there is too much space between the lid and the meat.
- Easy to prepare and pop in the oven.
- Tip for leftovers: Use for Mexican food for fusion meals (like the Big Burrito Board on page 73).

Tortellini Pea and Pancetta Pasta

I first enjoyed this dish in Venice, Italy, years ago. Its brilliant simplicity made such an impression that I made it myself as soon as I got home. I adapted the recipe by adding pancetta instead of ham, since it adds a bit more bite and saltiness to contrast the crisp peas. I also added shallots, white wine for sweetness and depth of flavor, and dill for freshness. If you make this with store-bought tortellini, you'll have a weeknight meal in no time.

Serves 2–4 | Prep time: 5 minutes | Cook time: 30 minutes

8 oz (225 g) pancetta

1 medium shallot, minced

2 teaspoons all-purpose flour

2 tablespoons (30 ml) dry white wine

½ cup (120 ml) heavy cream

1 cup (150 g) fresh or frozen peas

½ cup (50 g) Parmesan cheese, grated

12–16 oz (340–445 g) small cheese or spinach tortellini

1 tablespoon (15 ml) lemon juice

⅓ cup (21.3 g) fresh dill or parsley

1. In a medium skillet, add the pancetta. Bring the heat to medium-low and cook for 10 minutes. Once the pancetta is mostly cooked, add the shallots and cook for 6–8 minutes more, until translucent and softened. Stir in the flour, cooking for 1 minute. Stir in the white wine and cook for 2 minutes. Add the heavy cream and increase the heat to bring the sauce to a boil, then lower to medium-low and reduce until thickened, 5–7 minutes. Stir in the peas and Parmesan, then take off the heat and set aside.

2. Cook the tortellini according to the package directions; the time will depend on the size of the pasta. Just make sure to cook al dente, because it will continue to cook when mixed with the sauce. When the pasta is almost done cooking, reserve ¾ cup (175 ml) of pasta water. Drain the tortellini and return to the pot. Pour in the cream sauce, reserved pasta water and lemon juice; mix until thick and glossy. Just before serving, stir in the dill and serve warm.

Mahi Mahi Fish Taco Board

Fish recipes are always in my weeknight dinner arsenal; fish is a healthy dinner staple that takes very little time to marinate, cooks in an instant, and allows me to have dinner on the table in 30 minutes or less. This board, if you make the suggested Corn and Cabbage Chipotle Slaw and the Saffron-Honey Pickled Red Onions, takes a bit more preparation, but the vibrant, nutritious result is well worth it. As always, if you're short on time, buy premade pickled red onions and store-bought slaw; just add a dash of chipotle chili powder to spice it up. This board can also be made into a fish taco bowls board by swapping the tortillas for Tex-Mex Rice and/or chopped romaine lettuce.

Made on a 20" (51 cm) board

FOR THE BOARD

½ recipe Corn and Cabbage Chipotle Slaw (recipe on the next page)

½ cup (130 g) salsa

½ cup (112.5 g) guacamole

⅓ cup Pickled Red Onions (recipe on page 43)

4 cups (128 g) tortilla chips

lime wedges

2–4 servings of tropical fruits: papaya, mango, kiwi

4–6 toasted corn tortillas, steamed or toasted

NOTES

- Before making the fish, be sure to prepare ½ Corn and Cabbage Chipotle Slaw (page 42), and the Saffron-Honey Pickled Red Onions recipe (page 43).
- Halve the amount of chipotle in the slaw if you're sensitive to heat.
- Cut the fish filets in half before cooking.
- You can use any firm, white-flesh fish. Note that the cook time may vary, depending on the thickness of the filet.

Mahi Mahi Fish Tacos

Serves 4 | Prep time: 15 minutes | Cook time: 10 minutes

4 x 16 oz (455 g) mahi mahi filets, cut in half lengthwise to make 4 skinny filets

½ teaspoon salt, plus more to season

2½ teaspoons ground cumin

1 teaspoon smoked paprika

½ teaspoon chipotle chili powder

½ teaspoon ground cinnamon

¼ teaspoon white pepper

zest 1 lime (optional)

¼ cup (59 ml) neutral oil

1. Before making the fish, prepare the board with bowls of Corn and Cabbage Chipotle Slaw, salsa, guacamole, Pickled Red Onions, tortilla chips, lime wedges, and fruit. Leave a space for the fish and tortillas once they're done cooking.

2. Preheat the broiler to high, and line a small, rimmed baking tray with foil.

3. Rinse and pat dry the fish. Season both sides with salt; set aside on a paper towel-lined plate.

(continued)

4. In a medium bowl, combine the cumin, paprika, chipotle chili powder, cinnamon, white pepper, lime zest, if using, and oil. Dip the seasoned filets into the marinade, letting the excess oil drip off, and place on the foil-lined baking sheet.

5. Broil on high for 3–4 minutes per side; be aware that the cook time may vary depending on the thickness of the filet. When the fish is almost done cooking, toast the corn tortillas in a dry skillet.

6. Remove the fish from the oven and arrange, along with the warm tortillas, on the board. Serve immediately.

Corn and Cabbage Chipotle Slaw

If you're sensitive to spice, halve the amount of chipotle powder and add more as needed. You can also broil the corn cobs if making at home. Or, if you're in a hurry, use about 2 cups (260 g) of frozen corn instead of fresh for a quicker cook time—simply cook in a large skillet over a medium-high heat with 2 tablespoons (30 ml) of oil until golden brown.

Makes 4 cups (1.9 kg) | Prep time: 5 minutes | Cook time: 20 minutes

4 ears of corn, husked

½ cup (115 g) mayonnaise, divided

salt and pepper to season

1¼ teaspoons Dijon mustard

2 tablespoons (30 ml) lime juice (+ zest 1 lime)

1 tablespoon (20 g) honey

1 teaspoon chipotle chili powder

2 cups (140 g) purple cabbage, ¼" (6 mm) shredded

⅓ cup (5 g) cilantro, chopped

sprinkle of Cotija cheese

1. Coat the corn on the cob with ¼ cup (60 g) mayonnaise and season generously with salt and pepper. Heat a cast-iron skillet over medium-high heat. Add the corn, turning every 3 minutes or so, until golden and slightly charred. If needed, cover the pan with foil to lightly steam the corn. As the corn cooks for 15–20 minutes, make the slaw dressing (see below). Remove the corn and set aside to cool. Once cooled, cut off the kernels.

2. For the dressing, in a small mixing bowl, combine ¼ cup (60 g) of mayonnaise, the Dijon mustard, lime juice and zest, honey, and chipotle chili powder. Season with salt and pepper to taste.

3. Add the corn to a medium-size bowl, along with the cabbage. Drizzle with dressing and toss to coat. Gently mix in the cilantro. Sprinkle with Cotija cheese and a dusting of chili powder to serve!

Saffron-Honey Pickled Red Onions

Pickled red onions add crunch and an acidic pop to nearly anything you pair it with. Some of my favorite pairings are tacos, rice bowls, gyros, sandwiches, hotdogs, and more. Serve this with Lobster Rolls, Fish Taco Board, Burrito Board, Hotdog Board, Shaved Beef Gyro Board, enchiladas, or al pastor tacos.

Makes 1½ cups (232.5 g) | Prep time: 5 minutes, plus at least 1 hour for resting time

½ cup (120 ml) strawberry rosé vinegar (or substitute ¼ cup [60 ml] apple cider vinegar and ¼ cup [60 ml] champagne vinegar)

¼ cup (85 g) saffron-infused honey (or substitute regular honey)

1 teaspoon kosher salt, plus more to taste

1 red onion, sliced ¼" (6 mm) thick

1. In a medium, microwave-safe bowl, combine the vinegar, honey, and salt. Heat for 1–2 minutes until the honey dissolves, then whisk together. Stir in the onions and taste for salt. Let sit for at least 1 hour before serving (preferably overnight) for best flavor.

Chai-spiced Sawdust Pudding

(Vanilla Chai-spiced Portuguese Serradura Pudding)

Serradura, Portuguese for sawdust, is a secret weapon recipe. The individual servings make it perfect for both the proactive and procrastinatory entertainer; it can be made the day before, or the morning of. I adapted the recipe by adding chai spices, vanilla, and a bit of salt. If these flavors don't interest you, skip the spices and salty hints, and stick to the deliciously simple recipe of whipped cream, sweetened condensed milk, vanilla, and crushed cookies.

Serves 2–4 | Prep time: 10 minutes | Refrigeration time: 4–24 hours

---

1¼ cup (90 g) graham crackers or other sweet, dry cookies

pinch of salt

2¼ cups (535 ml) heavy cream

⅓ cup (77 g) sour cream or crème fraîche

10 oz (285 ml) can sweetened condensed milk

2½ teaspoons vanilla extract

1¼ teaspoons ground cinnamon

1 teaspoon ground cardamom

¼ heaping teaspoon ground ginger

¼ teaspoon ground cloves

generous pinch of kosher salt

1. In a food processor, pulse together the cookies and a pinch of salt until fine like sand. Set aside. This can also be done by hand, crushing the cookies in a plastic bag with a rolling pin.

2. Use a stand mixer, or hand mixer, with a whisk attachment to beat the cream to medium peaks. Add the sour cream, condensed milk, vanilla, spices, and salt. Continue whipping until medium stiff peaks form; 4–6 minutes total.

3. Using a zip-top bag (or a pastry bag), spoon in the whipped cream and snip a ¾" (2 cm)-wide hole at the corner. Pipe the cream into a single layer into individual 10–12 ounce glasses, jars, or other single serving vessels. Top with a ¼" (6 mm) layer of crushed cookies, followed by another layer of cream. Repeat this layering process until there are 2–4 layers of spiced cream and cookies—ending with a final layer of spiced cream. Carefully cover and let sit in the refrigerator at least 4 hours—preferably, overnight.

4. To serve, top with berries and a drizzle of Raspberry Pineapple Coulis (page 87), if desired.

Salted Brown Sugar Ice Cream

Growing up, my mom used to make a large batch of her vanilla ice cream for summertime gatherings. For years, I carried on her traditional recipe, even using her vintage ice-cream machine that required a bag of ice and a box of rock salt. Nowadays, ice-cream makers look a little different, so this recipe is a modern adaptation inspired by my mom's salty-sweet ice cream.

Makes 1 quart (946 ml) | Prep time: 10 minutes | Cook time: 5–7 minutes | Churn time: varies on ice-cream machine, about 30 minutes, plus 4 hours in the freezer

5 egg yolks

½ cup (115 g) brown sugar

1½ cups (355 ml) whole milk

1½ cups (355 ml) heavy cream

¾ teaspoon kosher salt

1 teaspoon vanilla bean paste

1 teaspoon vanilla extract

1. In a large saucepan, combine the egg yolks and sugar. Use an electric mixer and beat until pale yellow and thickened—4 minutes. Whisk in the milk, heavy cream, and salt, vanilla bean paste, and vanilla extract; bring the heat to medium-low. Stir constantly, until thick enough to coat the back of a spoon, about 5 minutes.

2. Strain the custard and refrigerate until completely cooled, at least 3 hours, preferably overnight.

3. Transfer the custard to an ice-cream machine and make according to machine directions; this should take about 30 minutes. Once churned, transfer to a container and freeze for at least 4 hours.

NOTES

- If you don't have vanilla bean paste, substitute 1 tablespoon (15 ml) vanilla extract.
- The churn time in the machine will vary, but it should take about 30 minutes. Keep an eye on the custard as it churns. Because this custard is very rich, if left too long, it can become very thick and buttery.
- If you're wanting to scoop the ice cream or make Fudgy Brownie Ice Cream Sandwiches (see page 93), transfer the churned ice cream to a container and freeze for at least 3 hours until hardened.

Cherry Rhubarb Poppy Seed Cobbler

Blueberry cobbler is one of the most popular recipes on my blog. Many people are surprised to read that you pour a whole cup (235 ml) of boiling water over the batter before putting it in the oven. The magic trick of this cobbler going into the oven soaking wet and coming out with a crunchy top is part of what I love about this recipe. To challenge the sweetness of the batter and berries, I use tart rhubarb, cherries, and poppy seeds for a bit of texture. This recipe is incredibly versatile and can be made with four cups of just about any fruit, so feel free to bake this cobbler with whatever fruit is in season.

Serves 4–6 | Prep time: 15 minutes | Cook time: 40–45 minutes

FRUIT MIXTURE

2 cup (200 g) rhubarb, cut 1" (2.5 cm) thick

2 cup (310 g) pitted cherries, fresh or frozen

2 tablespoons (30 ml) lime juice

1 tablespoon (9 g) poppy seeds

¼ cup (50 g) white sugar

2 tablespoons (16 g) cornstarch

BATTER AND SUGAR TOPPING

3 tablespoons (42 g) butter, melted

⅓ (67 g) + ¼ cup (50 g) white sugar, divided

½ cup (120 ml) milk, warmed

1 teaspoon vanilla extract

¼ teaspoon hazelnut or almond extract

1 cup (125 g) all-purpose flour

1 teaspoon baking powder

½ teaspoon kosher salt

1 tablespoon (8 g) cornstarch

1 cup (235 ml) boiling water

MAKE THE MIXTURE

1. Preheat the oven to 375°F (190°C, or gas mark 5) and grease an 8" x 8" (20 x 20 cm) baking dish.

2. In a medium mixing bowl, combine the rhubarb, cherries, lime juice, poppy seeds, sugar, and cornstarch. Toss to coat, then transfer to the baking dish.

MAKE THE BATTER AND TOPPING

3. In a medium mixing bowl, combine the melted butter, ⅓ cup (67 g) sugar, warmed milk, vanilla extract, and the hazelnut extract, whisking to combine. In a separate bowl, combine the flour, baking powder, and salt. Pour the dry ingredients into the wet and mix until just combined. Pour and spread the batter over the fruit.

4. In a small bowl, combine the cornstarch and ¼ cup (50 g) of sugar. Sprinkle the mixture over the batter. Bring 1 cup (235 ml) of water to a boil and pour over the entire cobbler.

5. Bake for 40–45 minutes, until the top is crisp and lightly browned, and the sides are bubbling.

6. Allow to cool for 10 minutes before serving with vanilla ice cream.

Mini Chocolate Chip Meringue Board

Meringue's piquantly sweet nature makes it perfect for all sorts of acidic, tart, and rich toppings. This book has many toppings to refer to, so use it as a resource for recipes and ideas. My favorite toppings are the Creamy Vanilla Lemon Curd and Tangy Whipped Cream because they cut through the sweetness of the meringue, but Chocolate Mocha Ganache works just fine too! If you're baking six smaller meringues instead of four, decrease the cooking and cooling time to 25 minutes.

Made on a 12" x 24" (30 x 60 cm) board

MERINGUE BOARD

⅓ cup (36.7 g) toasted chopped almonds

½ cup (40 g) toasted coconut flakes

1 recipe Vanilla Bean Macerated Strawberries

½ cup (119 g) Creamy Vanilla Lemon Curd (page 91)

3–4 cups (435–580 g) fresh fruit (kiwis, blueberries, strawberries)

⅓ cup (37) chopped, toasted pecans

½ cup (140 g) Chocolate Mocha Ganache (page 52)

½ recipe Raspberry Pineapple Coulis (page 87)

NOTES

- Make sure the egg whites are room temperature. If needed, fill a bowl with water that is hot to the touch. In a smaller metal bowl, one that can fit inside the bowl with the warm water, add the egg whites. Place the small bowl into the large and swirl the egg whites around until they come to room temperature.

- Use caster sugar for a smooth meringue.

- Make sure all bowls and measuring cups are grease-free, only use glass or metal bowls, and don't use any rubber spatulas until the meringue is whipped—any oil that gets into the egg whites will deflate them.

- To know you've reached stiff peaks, pull the beater out of the bowl and hold upright; the tips of the peaks should have only the slightest curve at the very top.

- Because meringue is finicky and deflates easily, the chocolate is carefully added in when the meringue is portioned out; this starts with half of the meringue portioned into four to six dollops, followed by a generous sprinkle of chocolate, the remaining meringue dolloped on top, and another sprinkle of chocolate that is carefully swirled in with a wooden skewer.

Vanilla Bean Macerated Strawberries

Makes 1 cup | Prep time: 2 minutes | Cool time: 1–24 hours

1 cup (170 g) strawberries, roughly chopped

1 teaspoon lemon juice

¼ teaspoon lemon zest (optional)

3 tablespoons (39 g) white sugar

⅛ teaspoon orange blossom water (optional)

¼ teaspoon vanilla bean paste or ¼ teaspoon vanilla extract

1. In a small mixing bowl, add the strawberries, lemon juice, zest, sugar, orange blossom water, and vanilla bean paste; toss and let sit for at least 1 hour, or preferably overnight in the refrigerator.

Chocolate Mocha Ganache

Makes ½ cup (120 ml) | Prep time: 2 minutes | Cook time: 5 minutes

½ cup (120 ml) heavy cream

pinch of salt

½ teaspoon espresso powder

4 oz (115 g) 70 percent dark chocolate, finely chopped

1. Add the heavy cream, salt, and espresso powder to a saucepan over medium-low heat, until it just begins to simmer (not boil). In a medium mixing bowl, add the finely chopped chocolate. Pour hot heavy cream over the chocolate and mix together until chocolate has melted. Set aside and allow to cool. If you make this the day before serving the meringues, place on a double boiler with a tablespoon more of whipped cream and mix until melted.

Chocolate Chip Meringue

Serves 4 | Prep time: 15 minutes | Cook time: 30 minutes, plus 30-minute cool time

½ cup (100 g) caster sugar (superfine sugar)

1 teaspoon cornstarch

3 egg whites, room temperature

¼ heaping teaspoon white vinegar

¼ teaspoon salt

1 teaspoon vanilla extract

2 oz (55 g) bittersweet chocolate, very finely chopped

1. Preheat the oven to 275°F (140°C, or gas mark 1). Line a large sheet tray with parchment paper.

2. Mix the sugar and cornstarch together and set aside. In a stand mixer, beat the egg whites on medium-high speed until foamy with soft peaks, 2–3 minutes. Once frothy, begin adding the sugar mixture about 1 tablespoon (13 g) at a time, waiting at least 30 seconds in between each addition—don't add too much at once, as the eggs will deflate. Once the sugar has been incorporated, add the vinegar, salt, and vanilla. Increase speed to high and beat until stiff peaks form, 5–8 minutes.

3. Divide half of the meringue onto the baking sheet in four to six dollops (depending on how many people you're serving), spaced a few inches apart. Make a slight crater in the center of each and sprinkle with about 2 teaspoons of finely chopped chocolate. Scoop the remaining meringue on top, create a small crater, and sprinkle with the remaining chocolate. Use a wooden skewer to swirl the chocolate into the meringue; spread the dollops slightly to reach 2–3" (5–7.5 cm) in diameter. Finish by creating a crater in the center with the back of a spoon.

4. Bake for 25–30 minutes, then turn off the oven and let sit for 25–30 minutes more before removing and letting cool completely.

Feeding a Crowd: Recipes for Gathering

Seafood Niçoise Charcuterie

Niçoise salads always remind me of springtime. This is a niçoise meal turned appetizer board. While my version deviates from the traditional salad, any of the ingredients can be substituted for other seasonal vegetables, seafood, or cheeses. This board pairs nicely with a chilled bottle of white wine.

Serves 6–8 | Prep time: 20 minutes | Make on a 12" x 36" (30 x 76 cm) board

FOR THE BOARD

5 oz (140 g) smoked salmon filet, flaked apart

8 oz (225 g) cooked jumbo shrimp

10 oz (280 g) Greek feta cheese (block form), cut into 10–12 cubes

¼ lb. (115 g) soft mushroom Brie cheese

8 oz (225 g) steamed and peeled baby beets, cut into 10–12 cubes

8 oz (225 g) cherry tomatoes

8 oz (225 g) haricots vert (green beans), trimmed, blanched

3 Belgian endives, separated

5 oz (140 g) grilled artichoke hearts, drained and quartered

4 oz (115 g) Kalamata olives

4 oz (115 g) Norwegian crispbread (or other seed crackers)

4 oz (115 g) water crackers

5–6 soft-boiled eggs

3 oz (85 g) rosemary Marcona almonds

¾ cup (169 g) creamy dill dressing or dip

½ cup (120 ml) green goddess dressing or dip

fresh dill to garnish

1. Start by putting down the bowls. Then place the other ingredients around them in curved lines and other patterns.

NOTES

- Great for a lunch or appetizer board.

- Add more veggies, like roasted carrots, blanched asparagus, and fingerling potatoes, if you have vegetarian guests.

- For soft-boiled eggs, boil for 7 minutes, then transfer to an ice bath to cool completely before peeling.

- Make sure to blanch the veggies in salted water for maximum flavor.

- Make the board your own work of art! I arranged the endives in the shape of a flower, and the feta and beets in a checkerboard pattern, but you can style the food however is best for you and your schedule.

Cinnamon Orange Sticky Buns with Orange Cream Cheese Frosting

In my house, a great brunch meal has both something savory, like bacon, eggs, or sausage, and something sweet, like these Cinnamon Orange Sticky Buns. This recipe gives two bread options: one with frozen, yeasted dinner rolls for a fluffier final product and one with quick-to-bake, canned biscuits for a faster, more buttery finish. Whichever dough base you choose, these buns will be the talk of the meal, especially with a gooey smear of tangy Orange Cream Cheese Frosting melting on top.

Serves 6–8 | Prep time: 1 hour (only 20 minutes prep time if using canned biscuit dough) | Cook time: 25–35 minutes

ORANGE CREAM CHEESE FROSTING

8 oz (225 g) cream cheese, room temperature

⅓ cup (77 g) sour cream room temperature

1½ cup (90 g) powdered sugar

1½ tablespoons (9 g) orange zest, 1 large orange

¼ teaspoon almond extract (optional)

ORANGE CINNAMON STICKY BUNS

32 oz (907 g) frozen yeast dinner rolls (about 12), thawed and risen once, or 32 oz (905 g) canned biscuit dough

MAPLE PECAN GLAZE

¾ cup (170 g) brown sugar

⅔ cup (167 g) unsalted butter, melted plus 2 tablespoons (28 g) softened butter to grease pan

⅓ cup (161 g) maple syrup or (115 g) honey

pinch of salt

1 cup (110 g) toasted, chopped pecans

ORANGE SPICED SUGAR

⅔ cup (133 g) white sugar

MAKE THE FROSTING

1. In a medium mixing bowl using a hand mixer, beat the cream cheese until smooth. Slowly beat in the sour cream, powdered sugar, orange zest, and almond extract until creamy. Cover and refrigerate until ready to use.

MAKE THE BUNS

2. Grease the sides of a 9" x 13" (23 x 33 cm) baking dish with 2 tablespoons (28 g) butter.

3. In a heatproof bowl, whisk together the brown sugar, melted butter, maple syrup, and a pinch of salt. Microwave until syrupy and warm, about 1–2 minutes, and pour into the baking dish. Sprinkle with the pecans and set aside.

4. In a wide bowl large enough to toss the dough in sugar, whisk together the sugar and cinnamon, until combined, then add 1 tablespoon (6 g) orange zest, a pinch of allspice and kosher salt. Mix until fragrant. Set aside.

5. Preheat the oven to 350°F (180°C, or gas mark 4).

6. If using frozen dinner rolls, allow the rolls to thaw and rise, then thoroughly toss and coat in the orange-spiced sugar. Arrange on top of the maple glaze, cover, and allow to rise in a warm area of your kitchen, about 30–45 minutes, or until they double in size. Once risen, sprinkle the tops with 2–3 more

1 teaspoon ground cinnamon

2 tablespoons (12 g) orange zest (1½ large oranges)

pinch of ground allspice

½ teaspoon kosher salt

tablespoons (12–18 g) of orange sugar, and bake on the center rack for 25–35 minutes, until golden on top and bubbling on the sides.

7. For the canned biscuit dough, shape each biscuit into a ball, and toss in the sugar. Arrange in the pan and bake immediately, until the sides are bubbling, and the tops are golden, 14–16 minutes.

8. Once the rolls are baked, remove from the oven and flip onto a serving dish, making sure to leave the pan on top as it cools, 10 minutes. Serve warm, with dollops of Orange Cream Cheese Frosting spread on top.

Mushroom, Bacon, and Cream Baked Eggs

If you think eggs cooked in butter are decadent, try baking your eggs in an ocean of salty bacon, sweet shallots, meaty mushrooms, and lush heavy cream. Not only is this breakfast rich and satiating, but it can also be whipped up in a matter of minutes. The eggs can be eaten à la carte or scooped onto your choice of bread.

Serves 2–4 | Prep time: 10 minutes | Cook time: 25 minutes

4 oz bacon (115 g or about 4 strips) thin cut, chopped

1 shallot, minced (optional)

salt and pepper to taste

6 oz (168 g) cremini mushrooms, sliced and roughly chopped

3 tablespoons (45 ml) white wine (optional)

½ cup (120 ml) heavy cream

4–6 eggs

1 cup (112.5 g) shredded Gruyère or white sharp cheddar cheese

FOR THE BOARD

4–6 English muffins, toasted

2 muffins

1 large strawberry Danish

1 lemon and poppy seed scone

2 cup (290 g) blueberries

1 blood orange, cut into wedges

16 oz (455 g) whole strawberries

NOTE

- Because all ovens and broilers are different, keep a close eye on the eggs to make sure they are cooked to your liking—the times in the recipe are best for a runnier yolk.

1. Preheat the oven to 375°F (190°C, or gas mark 5).

2. Before the eggs are cooked, gather the other board ingredients and arrange on the board.

3. In a cold, medium, ovenproof skillet, add the chopped bacon; bring the heat to medium-low. Render the fat for 4 minutes, then add the minced shallot and a pinch of salt and pepper; continue cooking for 5–7 minutes until the shallots soften and the bacon begins to brown. Add the mushrooms, wine, and more salt (if needed); scrape any brown bits off the bottom. Bring the heat to medium-high and cook off the wine, 3–4 minutes. Lower the heat to medium-low and add the heavy cream; bring to a simmer and salt to taste.

4. Carefully make wells in the cream and add the eggs, one at a time. Cover with cheese, avoiding the yolks if you'd like them to show in the final product, and place on the upper center rack of the oven for 5–6 minutes. Turn off the oven, crack open the door, and set the broiler to high, leaving the pan on the upper center rack. Broil until the edges bubble and the egg whites are just set, about 3–4 minutes for a runny yolk.

5. Remove from the oven and transfer to the board on a thick hot pad, alongside the other board ingredients. Enjoy the eggs hot, scooped onto English muffins.

Zucchini Fritters and Carrot Cake Fritters

Be warned . . . You won't be able to stop eating these. As you make these fritters, you may have the overwhelming impulse to bring the fritter to your mouth directly from the hot oil because yes, they are that delicious. Please heed my warning and let them cool for at least a few minutes before consuming. You'll thank me later!

Spiced Zucchini Kale and Gruyère Fritters

Makes 10–12 fritters | Prep time: 15 minutes | Cook time: 10 minutes

½ heaping cup (60 g) grated zucchini

1½ teaspoons salt, divided

canola oil or another neutral oil

½ cup (62.5 g) and 2 tablespoons (16 g) all-purpose flour

1½ tablespoons (9.5 g) curry powder

1½ teaspoons white sugar

¾ teaspoon baking powder

1 large egg

¼ cup (60 ml) + 2 tablespoons (28 ml) milk

1½ tablespoons (21 g) butter, melted and cooled

½ packed cup (33.5 g) Tuscan kale, finely chopped

½ cup (80 g) yellow onion, grated, excess moisture removed

⅔ cup (80 g) Gruyère cheese, grated

1 cup Cucumber Spicy Feta Dip (page 19) or other savory spread

1. In a colander, add the zucchini, and sprinkle with about ½ teaspoon (3 g) salt. Let drain for about 15 minutes, then squeeze out as much excess water as possible; set aside.

2. Add the canola oil to a large, high-walled skillet, until it reaches 2" (5 cm). Using a thermometer, bring the heat to 350°F (180°C).

3. Make the batter: In a medium mixing bowl, combine the flour, remaining 1 teaspoon (6 g) salt, curry powder, sugar, and baking powder.

4. In a separate bowl, whisk together the egg, milk, and butter. Mix the dry ingredients into the wet until just combined, then fold in the zucchini, kale, onion, and Gruyère.

5. Spoon about 1 tablespoon of batter (15 g) into the oil, making sure to not overcrowd the pan. Keep an eye on the temperature and adjust the heat as needed to keep it close to 350°F (180°C) at all times. Cook for about 2 minutes per side, or until golden brown.

6. Transfer to a paper towel-lined sheet tray, with a wire rack on top to drain off excess oil, and cool; serve immediately with your favorite dips and spreads.

(continued)

Carrot Cake Fritters

Makes 10–12 fritters | Prep time: 5 minutes | Cook time: 10 minutes

canola oil or another neutral oil

½ cup (62.5 g) all-purpose flour

½ teaspoon baking powder

¼ teaspoon baking soda

2 teaspoons ground cinnamon

1 teaspoon ground ginger

⅛ teaspoon ground allspice

¾ teaspoon salt

1 small egg

2 tablespoons (26 g) white sugar

1 tablespoon (15 g) brown sugar

½ cup (120 ml) buttermilk

1 tablespoon (14 g) coconut oil

1 cup (110 g) shredded carrots

¾ cup (110 g) mixed raisins

⅓ cup (37 g) roasted pecans, roughly chopped

½ serving Orange Cream Cheese Frosting (page 58)

1. Add canola oil to a high-walled skillet until it reaches 2" (5 cm). Using a thermometer, bring the heat to 350°F (180°C).

2. Combine the flour, baking powder, baking soda, cinnamon, ginger, allspice, and salt. In a separate medium mixing bowl, whisk together the egg, white sugar, brown sugar, buttermilk, and coconut oil.

3. Add the dry ingredients into the wet and whisk until combined, then add the carrots, raisins, and pecans.

4. Add a heaping spoonful, about 2 tablespoons (28 g), into the oil and cook until golden, about 2 minutes per side.

5. Transfer to a paper towel-lined, rimmed tray with a wire rack and let excess oil drip off. Serve warm, immediately after, with Orange Cream Cheese Frosting.

Breakfast Sammy Board

There are endless varieties of breakfast sandwich combinations. Some people prefer croissants, some bagels, and some English muffins. I prefer a big, buttery biscuit with a sweet-and-spicy sausage patty, crispy bacon, peppery arugula, a generous smear of jam, and a runny egg. So, this board is constructed to build *my* ideal breakfast sandwich, but you can switch up the ingredients to fit your own favorite. The possibilities are endless!

Serves 8–10 | Make on the 26" (66 cm) Big Board

FOR THE BOARD

6–8 Sweet-and-Spicy Sausage Patties

12 strips Honey Pepper Bacon

4–6 Miso Green Onion and Cheddar Biscuits (page 169)

3–4 plain bagels, toasted

3–4 English muffins, toasted

6–8 slices sharp white cheddar cheese

8–9 Danish and scones

1 avocado, sliced

1 small petite Brie cheese

1 cup (230 g) chive cream cheese, softened

honey

jam or jelly

4 cups (220 g) arugula

8 large strawberries

mixed fruit (kiwi, mango, orange, apple)

10–12 eggs, prepared to your liking

NOTES

- If you don't have a wire rack, add a sheet of well-greased foil to the baking pan when cooking the Honey Pepper Bacon.

- Other seasonal ingredients like fresh tomato can be added to the board.

- Simplify the board by buying premade, store-bought sausage, biscuits, and baked goods.

Sweet-and-Spicy Sausage Patties

Makes 6–8 patties | Prep time: 15 minutes | Cook time: 15 minutes

2½ teaspoons smoked paprika

¾ teaspoon white pepper

2 teaspoons dried sage

1½ teaspoons fennel seed

1½ teaspoons shiitake powder (optional)

4 teaspoons (20 g) brown sugar

1½ teaspoons kosher salt

1 lb. (455 g) ground pork

2 teaspoons canola oil

1. In a small bowl, combine the smoked paprika, white pepper, sage, fennel, shiitake powder, brown sugar, and salt.

2. In a medium mixing bowl, spread the pork into a single layer and season with the spices. Gently mix until the meat is seasoned. Wet your hands and shape into 6–8½" (15–21 cm) patties; set aside.

3. Preheat the skillet to medium and add a drizzle of oil. Add the patties, working in batches, and cook for 3–4 minutes per side, or until browned, glossy, and fully cooked to 145°F (63°C) in the center.

Honey Pepper Bacon

Makes 8 strips, serves 4 | Prep time: 5 minutes | Cook time: 30–45 minutes

8–10 slices thick-cut bacon, halved

fresh cracked black pepper, to season

2 teaspoons honey

1. Line a sheet tray with parchment paper. Grease a wire cooling rack with cooking spray then place it on the tray.

2. Lay the bacon in a single layer on the wire rack. Season with fresh cracked black pepper and flip. Drizzle the other side with a bit of honey and season with more fresh pepper.

3. Place on the center rack of a cold oven, then preheat to 350°F (180°C, or gas mark 4).

4. Depending on the thickness of your bacon and desired crispiness, cook for 30–45 minutes. Flip the bacon over 20 minutes into baking. Check for doneness every 10–15 minutes, until it is crisp enough for your liking.

5. Serve warm.

Broiled Al Pastor Tacos

Al pastor is a Mexican dish with Lebanese origins. Traditionally, the pork is roasted on a vertical spit like shawarma, and although not traditional, pineapple was added to this dish much later, and it enhances the flavors with acidic sweetness and tropical notes. My favorite ways to enjoy al pastor are burritos, tacos, quesadillas, and piled onto nachos with lots of melty cheese. The meat can be cooked on the grill, lending it smokey flavor, or, under the broiler if needed. Making the marinade is a bit labor-intensive if you're using dried chilis, but I promise you, the final product is worth it.

Serves 8–10 | Prep time: 45 minutes | Cook time: 20 minutes

FOR THE TACOS

2 dried ancho chilis, seeded

4 guajillo chilis, seeded

2 x 3.5 lb. (1.6 kg) pork tenderloin, silver-skin removed, halved lengthwise

salt to season

1 teaspoon black pepper, plus more to season

1.5 lb. (680 g) fresh pineapple chunks, divided

2 teaspoons lime juice

¼ cup (59 ml) neutral oil (grapeseed, canola, etc.)

2 tablespoons (40 g) chipotle sauce

1½ tablespoons (24 g) achiote (annatto) paste

6–7 cloves garlic

¼ cup (60 g) and 1 tablespoon (15 g) brown sugar

corn tortillas, toasted

fine-shredded purple cabbage

cilantro

fresh lime wedges

Oaxaca cheese or other melty cheese

1. Toast and soak the chilis: If you're planning to use canned chipotles in adobo, skip this step. In a large skillet, over medium-high heat, add the seeded, dried chilis to the pan. Let toast for 2 minutes, then flip and toast the other side until fragrant and slightly darkened in color, another 2 minutes or so. While the chilis toast, bring 3 cups (705 ml) of water to a boil. Add the toasted chilis to a bowl and pour over the boiling water; let sit until the chilis are softened and resemble wet leaves, 25–30 minutes.

2. On a cutting board, cover the tenderloins with plastic wrap. Using a meat tenderizer, flatten the meat into ½" (1 cm) thick strips. Season both sides with salt and pepper. Set aside.

3. In a food processor, combine 1 teaspoon (2 g) pepper, 8 oz ([225 g] about a quarter of the pineapple) pineapple chunks, 1 tablespoon (15 ml) lime juice, neutral oil, chipotle sauce, achiote paste, garlic, brown sugar, and a pinch of salt. Purée until smooth, 1–2 minutes.

4. Transfer the meat to a bowl and pour over 1 cup (237.5 ml) of marinade. Toss to coat and let sit for 20 minutes.

5. While the pork marinates, char the pineapple. Make sure excess liquid is drained from the pieces; if needed, blot with a paper towel. On a large foil-lined baking sheet, add the pineapple chunks and season with salt and pepper. Broil on high for 8 minutes until the edges are darkened.

6. Once the pork has marinated, transfer to the foil-lined sheet. Broil under high for 8 minutes until cooked and lightly charred.

7. Remove, let rest for 5 minutes, then roughly chop and toss with charred pineapple.

8. At this point, you can serve the al pastor on toasted corn tortillas with your favorite toppings, or you can add extra caramelization by frying it in a pan. To do the latter, add a drizzle of neutral oil to a large skillet over medium-high heat. Once hot, add the chopped pork and a few spoonfuls of the reserved marinade; cook until the edges are browned and caramelized; 3–4 minutes.

9. To make the tacos even better, heat a pan over medium-high heat. Lay down a tortilla and sprinkle with shredded cheese, add a portion of pork on top and allow the cheese to melt, making sure to let some of the cheese fry and brown directly on the skillet.

10. Serve warm with salsas, cabbage, lime wedges, and fresh cilantro.

NOTES

- The silver skin is the white, tough tissue that needs to be removed before cooking; to do this, slide a sharp knife just under the shiny, silver tissue on the tenderloin. As you cut, pull up on the tissue with one hand and carefully slide your knife away from you. Repeat until all tough tissue is removed.

- You can substitute four canned chipotle chilis in adobo for ancho chili and guajillo chilis.

- For the marinade, it makes 2 cups (475 ml). Only 1 cup (237.5 ml) is used for the marinade; the other is reserved for adding to the pan to refry the meat after broiling or grilling. The extra marinade can also act as a salsa.

- If you end up with extra marinade, you can freeze it for up to 3 months!

- If the sauce is too spicy, add ⅓ cup (52 g) more pineapple and 1 tablespoon (15 g) more sugar.

Peppers with Cream and Cheese

(Rajas con Crema y Queso)

Peppers in cream and cheese, known as Rajas con Crema y Queso in Spanish, is a popular Mexican dish from central and southern regions of the country. Commonly, the dish is made of strips of poblano peppers and onions, cream, and sometimes cheese and corn. As they cook, they fill your kitchen with intoxicating aromas guaranteed to make your stomach growl. To this adapted recipe, I add bell peppers, garlic, and a generous handful of sharp cheddar cheese at the end, but you can always substitute another cheese or skip that step altogether. This recipe can be served as a side dish with rice, on tacos or burritos, or add some cooked protein like shaved beef to make it part of the main dish.

Serves 6–8 | Prep time: 15 minutes | Cook time: 45 minutes

2 tablespoons (30 ml) grapeseed oil or other neutral oil

salt

2 poblano, cut into ½" (1 cm) strips

1 red bell pepper, cut into ½" (1 cm) strips

1 yellow pepper, cut into ½" (1 cm) strips

1 orange pepper, cut into ½" (1 cm) strips

1 yellow onion, cut into half moons

6 cloves garlic, minced

1 tablespoon (14 g) butter

¼ cup (60 ml) heavy cream

⅓ cup (77 g) sour cream

½ heaping cup (56 g) shredded sharp white cheddar cheese

1. In a large skillet, heat the oil over medium-high heat. Once hot, add the poblano, peppers, and onion. Season with salt and reduce heat to medium-low.

2. Cover with a lid for 20 minutes to soften the vegetables. Remove the lid and add the garlic and butter.

3. Continue cooking until softened, 20 minutes, stirring occasionally.

4. Add the heavy cream and sour cream and cook for an additional 5 minutes.

5. Remove from the heat and stir in the cheddar cheese until melted. Serve warm.

Big Burrito Board

(The BBB)

Mexico's rich cultural history has led to so much culinary crossover from other countries and regions—Mexican food is far more diverse than the Tex-Mex cooking often made in the United States. It is because of this culinary diversity that I include the Tamarind and Lemongrass Milk-braised Pork, a Southeast Asian-inspired dish. I'm certainly not the first to discover the delicious fusion of Asian and Mexican cuisine, but if you haven't thought of it before, try researching and experimenting with other flavor pairings on this burrito board.

Serves 6–8 | Prep time: 20 minutes (not including cooking ingredients; those times are listed on the individual recipes) | Made on a 12" x 36" (30 x 76 cm) board

¾ cup (86.7 g) red salsa

½ cup (60 g) Mexican crema

½ recipe Avocado Salsa Verde (page 78)

1 recipe Grilled Corn Pineapple Salad (page 77)

¾ cup (168.8 g) guacamole

1 cup (150 g) halved cherry tomatoes

½ cup (67.5 g) pickled jalapeño

2 radishes, thinly sliced

3 cup (165 g) spring mix

2 mangos, sliced

1 large lime, sliced

1 cup (55 g) shredded purple lettuce

8 strawberries

1 Cara Cara orange, sliced

1 cup (115 g) queso asadero or shredded mozzarella cheese

½ recipe Tamarind and Lemongrass Milk-braised Pork (page 37)

½ recipe Broiled Al Pastor Tacos (page 69)

½ serving Tex-Mex Rice (page 79)

½ recipe Rajas con Crema y Queso (page 71)

6–8 large flour tortillas

4 cup (128 g) blue corn tortilla chips

1. Arrange the fresh ingredients on the board: salsa, Mexican crema, salsa verde, corn pineapple salad, guacamole, cherry tomatoes, pickled jalapeño, radishes, greens, fruits, and cheeses.

2. Prepare and keep the proteins, rice, rajas, and tortillas warm until ready to plate on the board and serve.

NOTES

- While the recipes I have listed here are incredibly delicious, if you don't have time to make them, there are many easier substitutions, like seasoned ground beef, shredded chicken, refried beans, black beans, a meat alternative, or your favorite burrito protein!

- This board can be made from any and all premade ingredients—remember, it's more about the gathering than all the food being made from scratch.

- This board is served only with ½ servings of the recipes included. The other half can be reserved to fill bowls if you're serving a larger crowd, saved for leftovers, or you can just halve the recipes altogether.

Mexican-inspired Hotdog Board with Queso Dip

Hotdogs, depending on where you're from, have distinct ingredients and serving styles. I grew up with simple toppings of relish, ketchup, and mustard, but plenty more extravagant toppings exist. The regional inspiration for this board is obviously Mexico, but you can draw inspiration from any country and design your hotdog board accordingly.

Serves 4 | Prep time: 15 minutes | Cook time: 30 minutes | Made on a 12" x 36" (30 x 76 cm) board

FOR THE BOARD

4 brioche hotdog buns

4 (12 oz) jalapeño smoked sausage

½ Grilled Corn Pineapple Salad (page 77)

4 servings potato chips

CONDIMENTS

⅓ cup (45 g) pickled hot sweet jalapeños

⅓ cup (45 g) Pickled Red Onions (page 43)

¾ cup (75 g) guacamole

¾ cup (195 g) salsa

½ cup (112.5 ml) caramelized onion dip

¾ cup (106.5 g) red beet sauerkraut

GARNISH

1 Cara Cara orange, quartered

8 large strawberries

Three-ingredient Queso Dip (page 79)

1. Place the baskets, chips, dips, and toppings on the board before cooking the brats and queso. This will ensure that they are warm when the board is served, but just make sure to have a hot pad ready on the board for the queso because it will be very hot.

2. Grill the sausages according to the package directions and toast the buns. As the meat cooks, try to time the queso so that they're done at the same time.

3. Arrange the warm ingredients on the prepared board and serve immediately.

Grilled Corn Pineapple Salad

Corn on the cob smeared with salty butter and a few cracks of pepper is an American summertime staple, and for good reason. Its sweet and salty contrast is deeply satisfying; yet, with a few tweaks, it can be made even better. First, cutting the corn from the cob not only saves you a lot of dental floss, but allows each kernel to be tossed in salty Cotija cheese and soaked in the melty mayonnaise, pineapple-y, lime chipotle chili dressing that emulsifies when all the ingredients are mixed together. The inspiration for this salad is Mexican elote; without its genius, I wouldn't have discovered my favorite grilled summertime salad. I can also thank Mexican cuisine for the Avocado Salsa Verde (page 78), which can be paired with and spread onto nearly everything.

Makes 6–7 cups (825–960 g) | Prep time: 10 minutes | Cook time: 20 minutes

---

4–5 ears corn

¼ cup (60 g) mayonnaise

salt and pepper

1 jalapeño, minced

1½ cup (250 g) pineapple (.75 lb. [340 g] pineapple chunks)

3 tablespoons (45 ml) neutral oil

¼ tablespoon (4 ml) lime juice + zest 1 lime

1 tablespoon (7.5 g) ancho or Anaheim chili powder, plus extra for dusting

¾ cup (12 g) cilantro, chopped

5 oz (140 g) Cotija, crumbled (reserve 3 tablespoons [15 g] for garnish)

1. Preheat the broiler to high heat.

2. Coat the ears of corn with equal amounts of mayonnaise and season each ear with salt and pepper.

3. Put the corn on a baking sheet and broil for 12–15 minutes, turning every 5 minutes, until golden brown and slightly blistered.

4. Remove from the oven and cool; cut off the cob and set aside. Place in a medium mixing bowl and add the minced jalapeño.

5. While the corn is cooling, broil the pineapple on the same pan. Toss the pineapple in neutral oil, salt, and pepper. Broil on high for 6–8 minutes per side, turning once halfway through.

6. Once lightly charred, remove from the oven and allow to cool. Cut into bite-size pieces and add to the corn and jalapeño.

7. In a small bowl, whisk together the lime juice, zest, and chili powder. Pour over the corn and pineapple and toss, then add the cilantro and Cotija. Taste for additional salt.

8. To serve, garnish with more Cotija, cilantro, and a dusting of chili powder.

Avocado Salsa Verde

This Mexican salsa is like guacamole with a kick. It is citrusy, bright, and can be spread or drizzled onto almost anything that needs a touch of brightness and acid. Similarly, the grilled corn pineapple salad, inspired by Mexican elote, pairs well with almost anything. Both can be eaten by the spoonful, but I prefer serving them with chips or other main dishes, Mexican or otherwise.

Makes about 4 cups (1 kg) | Prep time: 5 minutes | Cook time: 20 minutes

24 oz (680 g) tomatillos, husked

1 jalapeño

3½ tablespoons (52.5 ml) lime juice

1½ teaspoons kosher salt, plus more to taste

1½ large avocados

2 oz (55 g) cilantro, stems included

1. Preheat the broiler to high heat.

2. Arrange the tomatillos and jalapeño on a sheet tray, and broil on high for 5–7 minutes per side, until blackened and blistered.

3. Remove the stem from the jalapeño along with the seeds, if you're sensitive to heat, and remove the hard stem bases from the tomatillos.

4. Transfer to a food processor with the lime juice and salt; pulse until puréed, then add the avocado and cilantro and pulse until smooth. Taste for salt and additional lime juice.

5. Serve chilled.

Tex-Mex Rice

I grew up with Tex-Mex cuisine, most of which is delicious, but I found the plain rice a bit of a disappointment. With the addition of a few flavor-packed ingredients, this rice works well as a side dish, but can also stand alone.

Makes about 6 servings | Prep time: 15 minutes | Cook time: 30 minutes

2 tablespoons (30 ml) olive oil

½ yellow onion, finely minced

1 jalapeño, finely minced

4 green onions (½ cup [52 g]), minced

generous pinch of salt

2 tablespoons (32 g) tomato paste

1¼ cups (197.5 g) white long grain rice

2⅓ cups (555 ml) chicken broth

1 tomato, chopped

1. Heat the oil in a rice cooker on sauté mode. When hot, add the onion, jalapeño, green onions, and salt. Sauté, stirring every few minutes, for 6 minutes. Stir in the tomato paste and cook for an additional 6 minutes.

2. Once the mixture caramelizes, add the rice and stir to coat. Pour in the broth, add the chopped tomato, and stir once more. Cook on the appropriate long grain white rice setting for your rice maker. When the rice is done, cover the rice cooker with a towel (this prevents water from dripping back on the rice).

3. Before transferring to a serving dish, fluff the rice with a fork.

Three-ingredient Chorizo Queso Dip

Here's a quick hot dip for when you have that cheese craving, with only three ingredients. We love this served with hotdogs, but it's great for any kind of dipping!

Serves 4 | Prep time: 5 minutes | Cook time: 7–10 minutes

1 large chorizo (¼ lb. [115g]), casing removed

5 oz (140 g) Oaxaca cheese, broken into large pieces

2 tablespoons (30 ml) light Mexican beer

1. Preheat the oven to 400°F (200°C, or gas mark 6).

2. In a 6" (15 cm) skillet, cook the chorizo on medium-high heat for 3–4 minutes, breaking it into smaller pieces as it cooks. Once cooked, add the cheese and beer; bake until gooey and bubbling, about 4–6 minutes. Serve and eat immediately; when the cheese cools, the dip will slowly begin to solidify.

Lemon Poppy Seed Biscuits

Strawberry shortbread is a favorite summertime dessert in my house, because it's so simple. I wanted to add some texture to the biscuit with poppy seeds, and of course, you can't have poppy seeds without lots of lemon! These drop biscuits take no time to make; however, the dough does need to freeze for 30 minutes beforehand to maintain its shape in the oven, so don't skip this step. Serve with the below lemon curd recipe, tangy whipped cream, and fresh strawberries—or try the Vanilla Bean Macerated Strawberries (page 52) and a drizzle of Chocolate Mocha Ganache (page 52).

Makes 8 biscuits | Prep time: 5 minutes, plus 30 minutes chill time | Cook time: 16–20 minutes

2 cups (250 g) all-purpose flour

2 tablespoons (30 g) brown sugar

3 tablespoons (39 g) white sugar

¾ teaspoon baking soda

1¾ teaspoons baking powder

2½ tablespoons (27.5 g) poppy seeds

1 teaspoon kosher salt

½ cup (112 g) unsalted butter, frozen and grated

1 egg, cold

1 cup (230 g) full-fat sour cream

½ cup (120 ml) half and half or whole milk

2 heaping tablespoons (12 g) lemon zest (about 2 medium lemons)

2 teaspoons vanilla extract

2 tablespoons (26 g) white sugar in the raw

1 serving Tangy Whipped Cream (page 90)

1 cup (145 g) strawberries

1 cup (145 g) blueberries

1 cup (237.5 g) Creamy Vanilla Lemon Curd (page 91)

1. Preheat the oven to 400°F (200°C, or gas mark 6) and line a large baking sheet with parchment.

2. In a large mixing bowl, whisk together the flour, sugars, baking soda, baking powder, poppy seeds, and salt. Add the grated, frozen butter and stir into the flour mixture. Use your hands to rub it into the dough until it breaks into larger, pea-size pieces.

3. In a separate medium mixing bowl, combine the egg, sour cream, half and half, lemon zest, and vanilla until smooth. Pour the wet ingredients into the dry ingredients and mix until the dough is just combined and has a tacky, thick consistency. Try to mix it as little as possible, of course, to keep the dough tender.

4. Prepare a plastic-lined plate or baking tray, one that will fit in your freezer. Using a spoon, divide the dough into 8 even biscuits. Place close together but not touching. Freeze for 30–35 minutes.

5. Transfer the cold biscuits to the prepared baking sheet, scooping the edges upward with a spoon to give them more height. Allow about 3" (7.5 cm) in between, as they will expand. Before baking, sprinkle with sugar in the raw, then transfer to the center rack of the oven. Bake for 16–20 minutes or until the tops are golden and crisp.

6. Allow biscuits to cool before serving with whipped cream, strawberries, blueberries, and lemon curd.

Toasted Coconut Guava Bread Pudding

Typically, when I think of bread pudding, I think of cold winter days. Because I love bread pudding so much, I wanted to make one that had flavors that pair well with warm weather. Here, the tart guava is balanced by nutty toasted coconut, warming cinnamon, and a melting scoop of vanilla ice cream. While this bread pudding is delicious served warm, it can also be served cold for hot summer days.

Serves 6–8 | Prep time: 15 minutes, plus 2–24 hours to soak | Cook time: 40–50 minutes

2 tablespoons (28 g) melted butter

1 tablespoon (15 g) brown sugar

1 cup (235 ml) sweetened condensed milk

1 cup (235 ml) full-fat coconut milk

2 tablespoons (28 ml) dark rum, or 1 teaspoon rum extract

1 tablespoon (15 ml) vanilla extract

2 large eggs plus 1 yolk

1½ teaspoons ground cinnamon

pinch of ground allspice

1 teaspoon kosher salt

1 cup (80 g) sweetened shredded coconut, toasted

12 oz (¾ lb. [340 g]) brioche bread, stale and cubed 1–2" (2.5–5 cm) thick

6 oz (175 ml) guava paste, cubed ½" (1 cm)

1. In a heat-safe bowl, combine the melted butter and brown sugar; 60–90 seconds, then pour into an 8" x 8" (20 x 20 cm), or similar-sized, pan and spread to coat the bottom. Set aside.

2. In a large mixing bowl, whisk together the sweetened condensed milk, coconut milk, rum, vanilla, eggs, yolk, cinnamon, allspice, salt, and shredded coconut. Add the stale bread cubes, along with the cubed guava paste, to the bowl, and gently toss to coat. Turn out into the prepared dish; cover and refrigerate for at least 2 hours, preferably overnight.

3. Preheat the oven to 350°F (180°C, or gas mark 4).

4. Transfer the dish to the center rack of the oven and bake for 40–50 minutes, until browned around the edges, but moist and custardy in the center. Let cool for 10 minutes, then serve warm with vanilla ice cream.

NOTES

- It is very important that the bread be very dry and hard. This can be done by baking it at 300°F (150°C, or gas mark 2) for 12–15 minutes.

- To measure the bread, look on the packaging for the ounces, or use a kitchen scale to weigh it.

- Toast the coconut in a single layer on a baking sheet, placed 2 racks under a broiler set to high, checking and stirring frequently, until golden brown and fragrant, 5–7 minutes.

Tiramisu French Toast

My husband's favorite dessert is tiramisu. He is very picky about what makes a good tiramisu. When my daughter Abby developed this recipe, she was afraid her dad might not be fully impressed. But I am pleased to report that this recipe has Paul's stamp of approval. He loved that the French toast gives the tiramisu an eggy, bread-puddinglike texture.

Because this recipe is labor intensive, it may be best made for a special occasion, or to surprise the tiramisu lover in your life.

Serving: 8–10 | Prep time: 30 minutes | Cook time: 2 hours, plus 24 hours to set and soak overnight

FRENCH TOAST IN COFFEE CUSTARD

¾ lb. (340 g) challah or brioche bread, sliced into 4" x 1" (10 x 2.5 cm)-thick strips, very stale

1⅓ cups (315 ml) whole milk, divided

2½ tablespoons (12.5 g) espresso powder

1 tablespoon (5 g) cocoa powder, plus more for dusting

1 cup (235 ml) heavy cream

2 large eggs, plus 3 large yolks

⅓ cup (80 ml) sweet vermouth

⅔ cup (133 g) white sugar

¾ teaspoon kosher salt

MAPLE MASCARPONE CREAM

5 large egg yolks

½ cup (100 g) white sugar

2 tablespoons (28 ml) sweet vermouth

½ cup (115 g) sour cream, room temperature

16 oz (455 g) mascarpone cheese, softened

¾ cup (175 ml) heavy cream, chilled

¼ cup (30 g) powdered sugar

2 teaspoons vanilla extract

1 teaspoon maple extract

3 tablespoons (42 g) butter, divided for batches

2 cup (475 ml) strongly brewed coffee

MAKE THE FRENCH TOAST

1. Let the bread strips sit out overnight, uncovered to dry out. If your bread is not stale before making the French toast, set the oven to 300°F (150°C, or gas mark 2) and place the bread onto a baking sheet. Bake until dry, 12 minutes. Let cool completely before soaking in custard.

2. In a small heatproof bowl, heat ½ cup (120 ml) milk until hot to the touch, 30–60 seconds in the microwave. Whisk in the espresso powder and cocoa powder until combined. Transfer to a large mixing bowl along with the heavy cream. Mix, then whisk in the eggs and yolks, followed by the remaining milk, vermouth, sugar, and salt. Mix until the sugar has dissolved.

3. Arrange the bread onto a 15" (38 cm) rimmed baking sheet. Pour custard over it and let sit for at least 1 hour to absorb, flipping the bread at least once for even custard distribution. It's preferable to cover the bread and refrigerate overnight.

MAKE THE MAPLE MASCARPONE CREAM

4. In a large mixing bowl, beat together the egg yolks and white sugar until pale yellow, thickened, and about doubled in size. Beat in the vermouth, sour cream, and mascarpone until smooth; set aside. In a separate bowl, whip the cream with the powdered sugar, vanilla extract, and maple extract, until stiff peaks form. Using a spatula or thin-edged spoon, fold the whipped cream into the mascarpone mixture, lifting upward and cutting through the center, turning the bowl a quarter at a time, until the whipped cream is just mixed in—do not overmix. Refrigerate until ready to use.

(continued)

NOTES

- Use whole loaf (.75 lb. [340 g] challah bread) sliced ¾" (2 cm) thick.
- Use decaf coffee if preferred.
- The bread needs to be pretty stale in order to absorb all of the delicious flavor and liquids.
- Save for a special occasion—not a quick recipe!

COOK THE FRENCH TOAST

5. When the custard has absorbed, heat about 1½ tablespoons (21 g) of butter in a large skillet over medium-low—alternatively, use a large griddle. Once the butter is melted and hot, working in batches, add half of the French toast. Cook 3–4 minutes each side, then remove from the pan and set aside. Make sure the heat of the pan isn't too high, as it will burn the sugar. Repeat, adding butter as needed, until all the French toast is made.

6. Once all the French toast is cooked, allow the bread to cool in the refrigerator, 30 minutes.

7. Once cooled, soak the strips in the coffee for about one minute. Let excess liquid drip off, then transfer to a 9" x 13" (23 x 33 cm) baking dish. Arrange the strips in a single layer, cover with half of the mascarpone cream, then add another layer of French toast strips. Finish with the remaining cream.

8. Transfer to the refrigerator and let sit overnight. To serve, dust the top generously with cocoa powder and serve on a pool of Raspberry Pineapple Coulis.

Raspberry Pineapple Coulis

Coulis is a simple, strained purée, and an easy way to add a new dimension to any dessert (or breakfast!). My favorite ways to serve it are on top of ice cream, brownies, pancakes, and plain Greek yogurt. Orange blossom water adds a complimentary, subtle floral note to the raspberries and pineapple. If you don't have it, just add a bit of orange zest, or skip it all together.

Makes 1 pint (475 ml) | Prep time: 5 minutes | Cook time: 10 minutes

1 cup (120 g) + 2 tablespoons (15 g) powdered sugar

¼ cup (60 ml) pineapple juice, or substitute orange juice

16 oz (3 cup) fresh raspberries

pinch of salt

2 teaspoon vanilla extract

¼ teaspoons orange blossom water (optional)

1. In a small sauce pot, combine the powdered sugar and pineapple juice over medium-low heat. Stir until the sugar begins to dissolve, about 3 minutes. Add the raspberries and warmed sugar blend to a food processor, along with the salt, vanilla extract, and orange blossom water. Purée until smooth; taste for additional sugar.

2. Pass through a fine-mesh sieve until all the seeds are strained. If the coulis is too loose for your liking, add it back to the saucepot over medium-low heat, and reduce until it reaches your desired consistency; it should be thick and a little viscous, like heavy cream. Serve warm or cold.

3. Store in the refrigerator.

Sour Cream Banana Cake

This banana cake recipe is near and dear to my heart. My mom used to make it for my sisters and me, and in turn, I've made it countless times for my family. This is a foolproof recipe that delivers a moist delicate cake for any occasion. If needed, this cake can also be made in a loaf pan without the whipped cream topping for a more casual presentation.

Serves 6–8 | Prep time: 10 minutes | Cook time: 45–55 minutes

1½ cups (187.5 g) all-purpose flour

1 teaspoon baking soda

1 teaspoon kosher salt

½ cup (115 g) sour cream, room temperature

1 tablespoon (15 ml) vanilla extract

½ cup ([112 g] 1 stick butter) butter, softened, plus more for greasing

1 cup (200 g) white sugar

2 eggs, room temperature

1 cup (300 g) ripe bananas, about 3 mashed

1 cup (110 g) toasted pecans or walnuts, chopped (optional)

4–5 strawberries to garnish

Tangy Whipped Cream (page 90)

NOTES

- Serve for breakfast or dessert.
- Classic *Reluctant Entertainer* family recipe.
- Delicious with chocolate ganache drizzle.

1. Preheat the oven to 350°F (180°C, or gas mark 4). Grease the bottom of a 9" (23 cm) cake or springform pan, and line with parchment.

2. In a small mixing bowl, combine the flour, baking soda, and salt. In a separate bowl, mix the sour cream and vanilla extract. Set aside.

3. Using a stand or hand mixer, cream together butter and sugar, starting on low speed and increasing to medium-high, until light, pale, and fluffy, about 3–5 minutes. Scrape down the sides of the bowl. Add in the eggs one at a time, and then the bananas. Scrape down the sides.

4. On medium-low speed, add half of the sour cream mixture. Mix for 30 seconds, then add half of the flour. Add the remaining sour cream, mixing until incorporated, then add the remaining flour; stop mixing when only a few streaks of flour remain. If you're adding nuts, add them to the batter and finish mixing by hand with a spatula. This alternating wet and dry ingredient ensures your cake remains extra tender.

5. Pour the batter into a prepared cake pan and bake on the center rack for 45–55 minutes, or until a cake tester comes out clean when inserted into the center.

6. Allow the cake to cool for 15–20 minutes before turning out onto a rack to cool. Let cool completely before topping with Tangy Whipped Cream, strawberries, and chopped pecans or walnuts.

(continued)

Tangy Whipped Cream

Whipped cream, as delicious as it is, is a very *one note* dessert. The addition of a tangy, acidic cream like sour cream, or even Greek yogurt, makes for a more multidimensional, refreshing dessert topping.

Makes 4 cups (800 g) | Prep time: 8 minutes

⅔ cup (160 ml) heavy cream, chilled

⅓ cup (40 g) powdered sugar

⅓ cup (77 g) whole-fat sour cream, crème fraîche, or Greek yogurt, chilled

¼ teaspoon kosher salt

1 tablespoon (15 ml) vanilla extract (optional)

1. In a medium mixing bowl using a hand mixer, beat the heavy cream and sugar to medium peaks. Add the sour cream, salt, and vanilla extract and continue mixing just until stiff peaks form. Refrigerate until ready to use.

Creamy Vanilla Lemon Curd

Lemon curd is a versatile dessert that should always be homemade. Prove me wrong, but I have never found store-bought lemon curd that doesn't have the texture of glue. The bright lemon flavor of this curd is warmed by vanilla extract, and the egg yolks lend a lusciously light consistency. Like butter, it melts in your mouth, leaving you wanting just one more bite.

Makes about 2 cups (475 ml) | Prep time: 10 minutes | Cook time: 15–20 minutes

½ cup (120 ml) lemon juice (3 large lemons)

1 packed tablespoons (6 g) lemon zest, from 2 lemons

½ cup (100 g) white sugar

¼ teaspoon kosher salt

6 large egg yolks

6 tablespoons (85 g) unsalted butter, cut into pats

1 tablespoon (15 ml) vanilla extract

1. In a double boiler, fill the bottom pot halfway with water and bring to a boil, then reduce the heat to medium-low. In the top bowl, whisk together the lemon juice, lemon zest, sugar, salt, and egg yolks. Stir frequently so the egg yolks don't curdle, 12–15 minutes, or until the mixture thickens and can coat the back of a spoon. The curd will continue to thicken off the heat. If the curd does not thicken within that time, increase the heat and give it 5–10 more minutes.

2. Transfer the curd into a separate bowl to cool; whisk in the butter, one pat at a time, and vanilla extract. Transfer to a jar and press the top with a sheet of plastic wrap. Allow the curd to cool before transferring and storing in the refrigerator for up to 3 weeks. You can also store the curd in the freezer for up to 6 months—just allow it time to thaw before you're ready to use.

Fudgy Brownie Ice Cream Sandwiches

Hands down, vanilla ice cream is my favorite summertime treat. My second favorite treat (for any season) is a dark, dense, fudgy brownie. If you don't have the equipment to make ice cream, or the time to make brownies, source both from the grocery—use 4 cups (560 g) of ice cream and one box of brownie mix. If you're looking to only make brownies, and not ice cream sandwiches, bake the brownies in a greased, parchment-lined 8" x 8" (20 x 20 cm) pan for 22–25 minutes.

Prep time: 10 minutes | Cook time: 18–20 minutes |
Ice cream sandwich assembly and freeze time: 10 minutes, plus 4–24 hours

¾ cup (167 g) butter

⅔ cup (58 g) cocoa powder

¾ teaspoon espresso powder

¾ cup (150 g) white sugar

½ cup (115 g) brown sugar

¾ teaspoon salt

1 teaspoon vanilla extract

2 eggs

¾ cup (94.8 g) all-purpose flour

⅓ cup (58 g) chocolate chips (milk or dark chocolate)

vanilla ice cream

MAKE THE BROWNIES

1. Preheat the oven to 350°F (180°C, or gas mark 4). Grease and line a 9" x 13" (23 x 33 cm) baking dish with butter and parchment paper.

2. In a medium skillet over medium heat, melt the butter. Once foamy, remove from the heat and stir in the cocoa powder and espresso powder until combined, then mix in the white and brown sugars for 2 minutes. Add the salt, vanilla extract, and eggs, stirring constantly until glossy and smooth, 2 minutes. Finally, add the flour and stir until combined—the batter will be thick and stiff. Pour the batter into the prepared dish and spread to the edges using a spatula. Sprinkle chocolate chips over the batter and bake for 18–20 minutes. Cool for 30 minutes before removing from the pan and transferring to a cooling rack to cool completely.

3. Let the ice cream sit a few minutes at room temperature to soften. Line a baking tray with parchment that can fit into your freezer.

MAKE THE ICE CREAM SANDWICHES

4. Cut the brownies down the center to make two 9" x 6.5" (23 x 15 cm) rectangles. Scoop the softened ice cream onto one brownie, so it is about 1–1½" (2.5–3.5 cm) thick. Top with the other half and use a spatula or offset spatula to smooth the edges. Transfer to the parchment-lined pan and freeze until the ice cream has hardened, at least 4 hours.

5. Divide the sandwiches into eight to ten bars. Serve bars cold from the freezer, because they will melt quickly.

CHAPTER 3

Go Explore: Recipes for the Great Outdoors

Grilled Shrimp Cocktail Skewers

Shrimp cocktail is a classic appetizer for any season. When camping in the summertime, shrimp is a filling protein you can grill and serve in a snap. When paired with a flavor-packed marinade and store-bought cocktail sauce, this appetizer comes together in a matter of minutes.

Serves 4–6 | Prep time: 10 minutes | Cook time: 5 minutes

12 large tail-on shrimp, deveined and patted dry

½ teaspoon salt, plus more to season shrimp

¼ cup (59 ml) olive oil

1 teaspoon fresh black pepper

2 teaspoons lime juice

zest of 2 limes, plus lime wedges to serve

4 large cloves garlic, crushed or minced

¾ cup (12 g) packed cilantro with stems, minced

6 oz (175 ml) cocktail sauce

1 tablespoon (5g) Cotija cheese or grated Parmesan

1. Season the shrimp with salt and set aside. In a large mixing bowl, combine the olive oil, ½ teaspoon (3 g) salt, black pepper, lime juice, lime zest, garlic, and cilantro. Whisk to combine, set aside about 3 tablespoons (45 ml) of the marinade, then add the shrimp and toss to coat. Spear two shrimp onto each small skewer.

2. Over a medium-high heat flame, cook the shrimp for 1–2 minutes per side, brushing with any excess marinade as they cook. Be careful not to overcook, and remember they will continue to cook a bit further off the heat. Remove from the heat, and plate along with a bowl of the cocktail sauce. Garnish with a squeeze of lime juice and sprinkle of Cotija; serve warm.

NOTES

- Search online for a tutorial if you need to devein the shrimp.
- Shrimp can be cooked over grates, or in a cast-iron skillet.
- When skewering the shrimp, I like to pierce through the top and the tail for two points of contact, as this makes flipping the shrimp easier.
- Soak wooden skewers beforehand if you're cooking the shrimp over an open flame.

Poolside Piña Colada Poptail Board

Ice pops are a staple of childhood summers. They are very nostalgic for me, so I wanted to make an adult-friendly version to revisit those summer days! Adding ice pops to iced rum on a sweltering summer day makes for the perfect "poptail"—as the ice pop melts, it turns the iced rum into a creamy piña colada, complete with a stirring stick. Just add a straw and sip away under the summer sun.

The board is composed of light, fresh ingredients with a bit of cheese for substance. If you want heartier ingredients, add meats, crackers, and salty nuts to make a complete charcuterie. I recommend using silicone molds because they make ice pop removal clean and easy. I've also found it helpful to make a batch or two in advance so there are always some in the freezer.

Made on a 20" (51 cm) board

FOR THE BOARD

2 Persian cucumbers, cut into spears

2 cups (290 g) blueberries

2 cups (290 g) strawberries

6 baby bell peppers, halved

1 cup (240 ml) green goddess dip

10 oz (280 g) feta cheese, cubed (substitute mozzarella)

2 large carrots, cut into spears

2 cups (130 g) snap peas

1 small Belgian endive

Piña Colada Sunset Pops

Makes 10 | Prep time: 15 minutes | Cook time: 6 hours to freeze

14 oz (425 ml) coconut cream

⅓ cup (67 g) white sugar

2 teaspoon vanilla extract (optional)

½ teaspoon kosher salt

1 heaping cup (165 g) fresh pineapple, ripe and cut into large cubes

1½ cups (255) strawberries, roughly chopped

8 oz (235 ml) white rum (or sub dark rum)

3 tablespoons (45 ml) lime juice plus slices

4 oz (120 ml) pineapple juice

ice

mint to garnish

1. In a blender or food processor, blend the coconut cream, sugar, vanilla, and salt on high. Pour out and set aside half of the mixture into a separate bowl. Add the pineapple to the blender and pulse two to three times—don't purée. Pour the chunky pineapple into the molds, filling halfway. Add the remaining coconut cream back into the blender along with the strawberries. Pulse until smooth; fill the remaining molds. Cover and add the ice pop sticks. Let freeze for at least 6 hours.

2. Before serving the poptails, mix together the white rum, lime juice, pineapple juice, and lots of ice; the cocktail will be strong, but will dilute as the ice pop melts. Garnish with fresh mint and lime slices.

3. Enjoy the ice pops in a glass with a good splash of the iced rum; as the ice pop melts, stir it into the cocktail.

Napa Valley Charcuterie Board

Earlier this year, my husband, daughter, and I visited Napa Valley with a mission to build an artisanal charcuterie board. We visited a local bakery for bread, and a few small grocery stores where we picked out local produce and received expert advice from cheese mongers and sommeliers for the best cheese, wine, and meat pairings. We got to taste cheeses we had never had before and learn about the intricate details of how they were made. If you're ever in Napa, I recommend taking the time to explore and learn more about the local purveyors. You'll gain a deeper appreciation for the food you're buying. A few of our favorite purchases were a blue cheese with whole juniper berries and a smokey sliced chorizo. We collected our artisan goodies onto the travel board, found a spot with wildflowers and a view looking into the hills, and ate, drank, and laughed until the sun set.

Serves 4–6 | Serve on the 12" x 24" (30 x 60 cm) Travel Board

---

.3 lb. (140 g) Montgomery's Cheddar Cheese

.2 lb. (85 g) The Blue Jay (by Deer Creek Cheese)

.2 lb. (85 g) Ossau-Iraty (French sheep milk cheese)

.2 lb. (85 g) Bel Canto (from Andante Dairy)

.2 lb. (85 g) Salami Francois

.2 lb. (85 g) Olympia Provisions Chorizo El Rey

.2 lb. (85 g) tarragon truffle Marcona almonds

strawberry rosemary jam

Epic Baguette from Buchon Bakery

½ cup (120 g) Kalamata olives

½ cup (120 g) green Castelvetrano olives

1 pear

1 green apple, sliced

strawberries

1 tangerine, for garnish

1 bottle of rosé wine

NOTE

- The perfect balance of cheese to use on a cheese board comprises three distinct flavors and textures: Cheddar cheese, blue cheese, a soft-ripened triple crème, made using pasteurized goat's milk with crème fraîche added to the curds.

Make-ahead Dill Bread

This recipe is adapted from Portland's *Palate Junior League* cookbook, and we've been making it for years. It's the perfect bread recipe to make ahead for a camping adventure. This bread is great for open-face breakfast sandwiches with eggs, bacon, lox and cream cheese, or a simple smear of butter.

Prep time: 2 hours (including proofing) | Cook time: 40–45 minutes

2¼ teaspoons dry active yeast

3 tablespoons (75 ml) warm water

pinch of sugar

⅓ cup (80 ml) buttermilk, room temperature

1 cup (225 g) full-fat cottage cheese, room temperature

2 tablespoons (26 g) white sugar

½ cup (80 g) finely diced yellow onion

1 tablespoon (14 g) unsalted butter, melted

⅓ cup (21.3 g) minced fresh dill (3 tablespoons [9 g] dried dill), packed

1½ teaspoons kosher salt

¼ teaspoon baking soda

1 egg, room temperature

2¼ cups (281.3 g) all-purpose flour

FOR THE BOARD

softened butter

flake salt

soft-boiled eggs

bacon

cream cheese

smoked salmon

fruit

1. Preheat the oven to 350°F (180°C, or gas mark 4). In a small bowl, pour the yeast over the warm water with a pinch of sugar. Gently whisk and let stand for 5 minutes until activated and bubbling. Grease a loaf pan with cooking spray; set aside.

2. In a large mixing bowl combine the buttermilk, cottage cheese, sugar, onions, butter, dill, salt, baking soda, egg, and yeast mixture. Sift in the flour in two to three portions, beating after each addition, until the dough forms a tacky, sticky ball; 6–8 minutes. Cover and let rise until doubled in size, about 1 hour.

3. Press the dough down and turn into a well-greased loaf pan. Let the dough rise another 35–45 minutes. Preheat the oven to 350°F (180°C, or gas mark 4).

4. Bake on the center rack of the oven for 40–50 minutes, until golden brown. Brush with butter and sprinkle with salt immediately after baking, then let cool for 15 minutes before removing from the pan.

NOTES

- Great for camping and hiking—you can make it up to 3 days in advance.

- Freeze and thaw; easy to slice for breakfast sammies.

Sunrise Board with No-bake Breakfast Bars

Who knew it could be so much fun to get up before the sun? Outdoor boards sometimes take a little planning ahead, so this time we made our breakfast bars the night before, gathered the other food, and set our alarms for 5:30 am. Well worth it, we'll never forget eating breakfast together as the beautiful sun peeked its way over the ocean at Duncan's Landing on the California coast.

Made on the 12" x 24" (30 x 60 cm) Travel Board

FOR THE BOARD

4 No-bake Breakfast Bars (½ recipe)

3–4 small Greek yogurt cups

16 strawberries

1 mango, sliced

2 cups (250 g) raspberries

1 orange, sliced

2 cups (274 g) cashews

12 dates

4 hard-cooked eggs, cut in half

5–6 mixed pastries

1 cup (100 g) large granola chunks

½ cup (130 g) peanut butter

½ cup (119 g) Creamy Vanilla Lemon Curd (page 91)

No-bake Breakfast Bars

Yields: 8 bars | Prep time: 15 minutes | Chill time: at least 2 hours

¼ cup (45 g) coconut oil

¼ cup (28 g) butter

⅓ cup (115 g) honey

½ cup (115 g) brown sugar

½ teaspoon kosher salt

2 cups (160 g) instant quick oats

1 cup (27 g) crisp rice cereal

¾ cup (60 g) sweetened shredded coconut, toasted

1 cup (110 g) toasted pecans, chopped

2 tablespoons (14 g) ground flaxseeds

¼ cup (44 g) chia seeds

1. Prepare an 8" x 8" (20 x 20 cm) pan with a sheet of parchment paper that overhangs 2–3" on each side.

2. In a small heat-safe bowl, combine the coconut oil, butter, honey, brown sugar, and salt. Melt in the microwave, heating in 30-second intervals, until the brown sugar begins to dissolve.

3. In a medium-size mixing bowl, add the oats, crisp rice cereal, coconut, and pecans.

4. Pour the butter mixture over the dry ingredients and toss to coat. Lastly, mix in the ground flaxseeds and chia seeds. Scrape the mixture into the prepared pan and press down (using another sheet of parchment paper), until compressed and flat on top.

5. Refrigerate at least 2 hours (preferably overnight) before cutting into eight bars for serving.

Shaved Beef Gyros Picnic Board

This board is very loosely inspired by the classic cold-weather pairing of grilled cheese and tomato soup. The board is obviously influenced by Arab and Mediterranean cuisines, with some nontraditional elements added, like the option to eat the beef on leaves of Romaine. The summery stars of the board, the Shaved Beef Gyros and the Chilled Cucumber and Fennel Soup, make a fresh and flavorful meal for a balmy spring or summer picnic. I recommend doubling the shaven beef recipe to keep for leftovers throughout the week—it is so easy to reheat on the stovetop and serve with wilted greens, basmati rice, and a drizzle of the umami-rich, garlicky Homemade Caesar Dressing (page 27).

Serves 4 | Made on the 12" x 24" (30 x 60 cm) Travel Board

FOR THE BOARD

1 recipe Chilled Cucumber and Fennel Soup

½ English cucumber, sliced

1 large tomato, sliced

4 servings cantaloupe

⅓ cup (52 g) Saffron-Honey Pickled Red Onions (page 43)

½ cup (112 g) hummus

½ recipe Cucumber Spicy Feta Dip (page 19)

½ cup (120 g) Kalamata olives

1 small head Gem lettuce or Romaine

1 small lemon, cut into wedges

½ cup (100 g) micro greens

4 servings pita or other flat bread

½ cup (75 g) crumbled feta

NOTES

- The soup should be made at least 4 hours in advance so it has time to chill. It can be made up to 3 days in advance.

- To seed a cucumber, cut it in half lengthwise and run a spoon down the center to scrape out the seeds.

- The Cucumber Spicy Feta Dip can be swapped with tzatziki sauce, fresh red onion can substitute for the pickled red onions, and other sides like tabbouleh, bean salads, or roasted potatoes can replace the soup.

Chilled Cucumber and Fennel Soup

Makes about 4 cups (946 ml) | Prep time: 5 minutes | Cook time: 15 minutes | Chill time: 4 hours, preferably overnight

¼ cup (59 ml) olive oil, divided

2 small fennel bulbs, diced

1¼ teaspoons salt, plus more to season and taste

4 cloves garlic, minced

1 small zucchini, seeded and cubed ¾" (2 cm)

½ teaspoon white pepper

2 Persian cucumbers, chopped into large pieces

1 avocado

2 tablespoons (30 ml) lime juice, plus more to taste (about 1 lime)

½ cup (115 g) Greek yogurt

⅓ cup (21.3 g) dill, roughly chopped

¼ cup (15 g) parsley, roughly chopped, plus a few leaves to garnish

2 stalks green onion

¾ cup (175 ml) ice water

feta to garnish

1. In a medium skillet, add half of the oil. Once hot, add the fennel and lower the heat to medium. Season with a generous pinch of salt and cook for 3 minutes, then add the garlic and cook until softened, 4 minutes more. Transfer to a bowl and allow to cool, 5 minutes. Heat the same pan over medium-high heat and add the remaining oil. Once shimmery, add the zucchini. Let sit, undisturbed, until browned, 2 minutes, then season with salt and toss; cook 1 more minute. Transfer to a bowl and allow to cool for 5 minutes.

2. In a blender, combine the cooled fennel and garlic, zucchini, salt, white pepper, cucumber, avocado, lime juice, Greek yogurt, dill, parsley, green onion, and ½ cup (120 ml) of ice water. Blend until smooth and taste for additional salt and lime juice. If the soup is too thick, incorporate 1–2 tablespoons (15–28 ml) of water at a time until loosened to your liking. Chill the soup for at least 4 hours before serving with feta and herbs.

Spiced Shaved Beef Shawarma

Prep time: 5 minutes, plus 30–45 minutes marinating time | Cook time: 10 minutes

4 teaspoons smoked paprika

1 teaspoon ground cinnamon

1½ teaspoons ground cardamom

2 teaspoons ground cumin

½ teaspoon cloves

3 teaspoons kosher salt, plus more to season the beef

1 teaspoon white pepper

1 lime, juiced (about 2–3 tablespoons [30–45 ml])

¼ cup (59 ml) and 2 tablespoons (30 ml) olive oil, divided

2½ teaspoons honey

1 lb. (455 g) shaved beef

1. In a bowl, whisk together the smoked paprika, cinnamon, cardamom, cumin, cloves, 1 teaspoon (6 g) salt, and white pepper. Whisk the lime juice, ¼ cup (59 ml) olive oil, and the honey until combined. In a medium mixing bowl, add the shaved beef and season with 2 teaspoons salt. Pour the spiced oil over and mix to coat. Refrigerate and let marinate for 30–45 minutes.

2. Once the meat has marinated, heat a large skillet over medium-high heat, and add the remaining 2 tablespoons (30 ml) olive oil. Once hot, add the shaven beef in a single layer. Cook, stirring occasionally, for 8–10 minutes, until the moisture has evaporated, and the meat begins to brown and darken around the edges.

3. If you're taking this meal on a picnic, make sure to have all the ingredients packed and ready to go before the meat is cooked. Bring the meat in a container wrapped in foil, to keep as much heat in as possible.

Berry Barbecue Chicken

Barbecuing marinated chicken thighs is a foolproof way to serve a crowd—their high fat content makes them nearly impossible to overcook. These chicken thighs are paired with a homemade, vibrant rosy-red barbecue sauce with sharp, citrus, berry, and chili flavors that are subdued by the sweetness of brown sugar and earthy spices. A Crunchy Kiwi Pecan Salsa (page 112) might seem like an unlikely pairing for barbecued chicken, but I assure you the buttery, warm pecans, crunchy red onion, grassy jalapeño, and cooling Thai basil pair deliciously with fatty chicken thighs and the sharp berry sauce. If the kiwis you have are well ripened, you may want to add a squeeze of lime juice to balance the sweetness.

Serves 2–4 | Prep time: 35 minutes, plus 8–48 hours marinating time |
Cook time: 12–15 minutes, plus 10 minutes to rest

6 chicken thighs, boneless and skinless

2 teaspoons kosher salt, plus more to season

½ cup (120 g) ketchup

4 cloves garlic

1 heaping cup (125 g) raspberries

1 heaping cup (145 g) strawberries, chopped

3 red Fresno red chilis (substitute with 1 serrano or jalapeño chili, seeded)

1 teaspoon lime zest

1 teaspoon orange zest

½ cup (120 ml) orange juice

⅓ cup (75 g) brown sugar

1 teaspoon ground cinnamon

1 teaspoon ground coriander

1 teaspoon ground cumin

2 tablespoons (40 g) pomegranate molasses

2 teaspoons black pepper

1 tablespoon (15 ml) lime juice

1 tablespoon (15 ml) white balsamic vinegar (substitute apple cider vinegar)

1 recipe Crunchy Kiwi Pecan Salsa (page 112)

2–4 servings grilled ciabatta bread to serve

SEASON THE CHICKEN

1. Season the chicken thighs with salt and pepper on both sides. Transfer to a resealable bag and refrigerate.

MAKE THE SAUCE

2. In a food processor, purée the salt, ketchup, garlic, raspberries, strawberries, chilis, serrano, lime zest, orange zest, orange juice, brown sugar, cinnamon, coriander, cumin, and pomegranate molasses until smooth. Set a fine-mesh strainer over a medium sauce pot and add half of the purée. Use a spatula to push the purée through, until the seeds are strained out. Repeat for the remaining purée. Add the black pepper to the sauce, and bring to a boil. Lower the heat to medium, and reduce for 15 minutes or so, until thick enough to coat the back of a spoon. Take off the heat and stir in the lime juice and white balsamic vinegar. Transfer to a bowl, and chill in the refrigerator until at least room temperature.

MARINATE AND COOK THE CHICKEN

3. Once the barbecue sauce has cooled, add 1 cup (250 g) to the chicken and mix until coated. Let marinate for 8–48 hours. Before grilling, let the chicken sit out for about 30 minutes, to come closer to room temperature. To cook, heat a grill to medium-high heat, grease the grates well, then add the chicken thighs with 2–3 tablespoons (30 to 45 ml) of excess marinade drizzled on top. Cook for

5 minutes per side, remove from the heat, brush with the reserved barbecue sauce, and let rest for 10 minutes.

SERVE THE CHICKEN

4. Serve the chicken warm with Crunchy Kiwi Pecan Salsa spooned over it, with a side of warm, grilled bread and butter.

Crunchy Kiwi Pecan Salsa

Serves 2–4 | Prep time: 10 minutes

⅓ cup (55 g) red onion, minced

2 teaspoons lime or lemon juice

pinch of salt

½ heaping cup (55 g) toasted pecans or walnuts, roughly chopped

4 kiwis, peeled and roughly chopped

1 jalapeño or 2 Fresno chilis, minced

1 teaspoon honey to drizzle

14 leaves Thai or regular basil, chopped

1. While the chicken rests, in a small mixing bowl, combine the red onion, lime juice, and salt. Let sit for 2 minutes. Add in the chopped pecans, kiwis, jalapeño, honey, and another pinch of salt. Mix, then toss in the basil. Refrigerate until ready to serve.

NOTES

- In the Crunchy Kiwi Pecan Salsa, the nuts aren't a necessity, but they do add a nutty, warm crunch. Additionally, the Thai basil can be substituted with regular basil, and the Fresno chili in the salsa and marinade can be swapped for a serrano or jalapeño—if you're sensitive to heat, just make sure to remove the seeds or omit it altogether. You can use nectarines or peaches instead of kiwi, as well.

- For the pomegranate molasses in the sauce, substitute with 2½ teaspoons (17 g) honey, 2½ teaspoons lime juice, and ½ teaspoon (2.5 ml) soy sauce.

- For best results, marinate the chicken 48 hours in advance.

- The chicken can also be cooked under a broiler set to high, on a foil-lined baking sheet, for 10 minutes, or until charred around the edges and cooked to 165°F (75°C).

Glamping Lobster Roll Dinner Board

We developed this board over the summer, while glamping at an Airstream camp near the Russian River in Northern California. This area is well known for their wine production, so to honor that, we wanted to make a fancy seafood meal to pair with our chilled bottle of Pinot Grigio. Luckily, glamping usually involves access to a grocery store, a stovetop, and a refrigerator to make such an elegant meal possible—we even brought our own candles, napkins, and tablecloth to level it up!

Made on the 26" (66 cm) Big Board

FOR THE BOARD

4–6 brioche rolls, or preferred type of bread

6–8 cooked lobster tails, halved (or 30 cups [4 kg] cooked lobster)

2 cups (950 g) Corn and Cabbage Chipotle Slaw

¾ cup (169 g) guacamole

½ cup (60 g) Cotija cheese

¾ cup Pickled Red Onions (page 43)

12–14 strawberries

1 mango, sliced

3 kiwis, sliced

½ cup (8 g) cilantro, chopped

1 head butter leaf lettuce

regular and blue corn tortilla chips

1 lime, cut into wedges

1 tablespoon (3 g) chives, minced to garnish

chilled Pinot Grigio to serve

NOTES

- Make the Corn and Cabbage Chipotle Slaw and Pickled Red Onions ahead and refrigerate. These need to be served cold for the best flavor.

- Before you start cooking the lobster, make sure the rest of the board is assembled so you can serve the lobster rolls warm.

- If, after reading the instructions, you're still confused about how to halve and cook the lobster tails, try watching an online video for visual instructions.

- If you're sensitive to spice, halve the amount of chipotle powder in the slaw and add more as needed.

- If you're looking to save time and energy, buy the slaw and pickled onions premade and the lobster precooked.

- If you're making this recipe at home, the corn cobs can be broiled; alternatively, use about 2 cups (260 g) of frozen corn instead of fresh for a quicker cook time. Simply cook in a large skillet over medium-high with 2 tablespoons (30 ml) of oil until cooked and golden brown.

Lobster Rolls

Serves 4–6 | Prep time: 15 minutes | Cooking time: 20 minutes

1½–2 lb. (680–910 g) lobster tails, halved (or about 30 ounces precooked lobster)

½ cup (112 g) butter

4 cloves garlic, minced

1 jalapeño, finely chopped

pinch of salt and pepper

4–6 brioche rolls, making a slit ¾ of the way through

1 head butter leaf lettuce

2 cups (950 g) Corn and Cabbage Chipotle Slaw (page 42)

Pickled Red Onions (page 43)

Cotija cheese

cilantro

PREP THE LOBSTER TAIL

1. Place the lobster shell side up. Place the tip of a sharp knife onto the center of the shell; carefully, cutting lengthwise, press down and cut through. Finish by cutting the tail completely down the center, so you're left with two separate halves.

COOK THE LOBSTER

2. In a small skillet, combine the butter, garlic, jalapeño, pepper, and salt over medium-low heat. Cook for 4–5 minutes until fragrant and infused. If the pan begins to smoke and the butter begins to burn, reduce the heat.

3. As the butter infuses, begin heating a medium-size cast-iron skillet over medium heat. For precooked lobster meat: Simply warm it and toss it in ⅛ cup (28 g) of the butter mixture, reserving the remaining butter to toast the bread.

4. Once the pan is hot, add some infused butter and add the tails, flesh side down. Add a few more tablespoons of the butter mixture and begin basting the lobster for about 2 minutes. To baste, tilt the pan slightly toward you, then use a large spoon to continuously scoop and spread the butter onto the tails. Once the flesh is visibly opaque and cooked about halfway, flip the tail over so the shell is against the pan and cook for another 1–2 minutes. When cooked, the flesh will become opaque, and the shell will turn a vibrant red—do not overcook the lobster; If the lobster has curled into an O shape, then you have overcooked it. Once cooked, remove from the pan and cover with foil to keep warm. Repeat this process for any remaining lobster tails.

5. With the remaining butter, toast the bread in the pan until golden.

ASSEMBLE THE LOBSTER ROLL

6. Place two leaves of lettuce on the roll, followed by lobster, corn slaw, pickled onions, Cotija, and a sprinkle of cilantro.

Sunset Sushi Beach Board

On a sunny Sunday afternoon, make this refreshingly easy edamame salad, grab some premade sushi from your favorite local spot, and head to the beach with loved ones for a stress-free dinner with a view.

Made on the 12" x 24" (30 x 60 cm) Travel Board

2–4 servings sushi (5–6 rolls)

12 chicken gyoza

soy sauce

wasabi

pickled ginger

6 ice cream mochi or other dessert

2 kiwis

1 cup (170 g) strawberries, sliced

1 apricot, sliced

mandarin orange to garnish

Citrus Edamame Cucumber Salad

Citrus Sesame Dressing

Citrus Edamame Cucumber Salad

Makes about 4 cups (120 g) | Prep time: 20 minutes

---

1 cup (170 g) edamame, fresh or frozen and thawed

3 Persian cucumbers, chopped

1 medium mango, julienned or chopped

1 red chili pepper, julienned (or substitute a mini red bell pepper)

1 cup (70 g) purple cabbage, finely shredded

2 tablespoons (5 g) Thai basil, chiffonade

2 teaspoons mint, chiffonade

1 cup (130 g) jicama, julienned or roughly chopped

1 cup (200 g) micro greens

1. In a medium mixing bowl, combine the edamame, cucumber, mango, red chili, cabbage, basil, mint, jicama, and micro greens. Serve with Citrus Sesame Dressing.

Citrus Sesame Dressing

Makes about ⅓ cup (80 ml)

1 teaspoon toasted sesame oil

2 tablespoons (30 ml) peanut oil, or neutral oil like grapeseed or avocado

1½ tablespoons (22.5 ml) rice vinegar

2 tablespoons (30 ml) grapefruit juice

1 tablespoon (15 ml) mandarin orange juice + ½ teaspoon zest

2½ teaspoons white sugar

½ teaspoon kosher salt

2 teaspoons white miso

3 tablespoon (24 g) toasted sesame seeds

½ teaspoon salt, plus more to taste

1. In a small blender or food processor, combine the sesame oil, peanut oil, rice vinegar, grapefruit juice, mandarin orange juice, sugar, salt, miso, and toasted sesame seeds. Blend until slightly thickened and lighter in color—season with more salt if needed. The dressing will be on the runnier side.

2. Toss the vegetables and herbs in half of the dressing, adding more as needed.

Pineapple Whip with Cookies and Salted PB Stuffed Dates

Being in the wilderness calls for relaxation and unwinding. While I love to cook and prepare food for others, sometimes, I just want a break. These campaign desserts are my go-tos for a quick, low-energy sweet treat. Before leaving for camping, I premake as much food as possible, including the whipped cream for this dessert. This way, I can throw everything together in 10 minutes or less. If you're looking to save even more time, substitute 2 cups (120 g) of Cool Whip for the heavy cream and powdered sugar—I do still recommend adding the sour cream, because it adds such great flavor, but you don't have to. Turn these recipes into a board by adding more premade dessert bites and drinks, like Cinnamon Vanilla Hot Chocolate (recipe on page 211).

Serves 4–6 | Prep time: 10 minutes

PINEAPPLE WHIP WITH COOKIES

1¼ cups (75 g) whipping cream

¼ cup (30 g) and 2 tablespoons (15 g) powdered sugar

2 tablespoons (30 g) sour cream (optional)

1 teaspoon vanilla extract (optional)

pinch of salt

½ cup (97.5 g) crushed pineapple, drained

SALTED PB STUFFED DATES

½ cup (130 g) crunchy, no-stir peanut butter

12 pitted dates

honey to drizzle

flake salt to sprinkle

powdered sugar to dust (optional)

2 tablespoons (10 g) toasted coconut to garnish (optional)

4–6 servings crunchy cookies

tea to serve

MAKE THE PINEAPPLE WHIP

1. Using a hand mixer, beat the whipping cream and powdered sugar until medium peaks form, then add the sour cream, if using, vanilla, and a pinch of salt. Beat to stiff peaks, then fold in the drained, crushed pineapple.

MAKE THE DATES

2. Using a spoon, divide the peanut butter into the existing split of the pitted dates. Drizzle each with honey, and garnish with a pinch of flake salt. Best with a dusting of powdered sugar.

3. Garnish the Creamy Pineapple Whip with toasted coconut, if you like, and serve cold with crunchy cookies, stuffed dates, and warm tea.

Field Day Chocolate Banana Pudding Board

In elementary school, field days were my kid's favorite day of the school year—and mine too. It meant that they would come home exhausted and hit the hay early and with ease. Beyond the welcomed exhaustion, field days were a great time for kiddos to move their bodies, play, and of course eat, outdoors. This board was inspired by a need for a fun and practical field day dessert, one that is kid-friendly *and* eco-friendly. Typically, wrappers instantly go into the trash after being used, so we wanted to give the snack bags a second life before tossing. Additionally, we used biodegradable and compostable bowls and plastic spoons to serve the dessert, in order to make the board as environmentally friendly as possible, while also eliminating dishes to wash. Eco-friendly products are becoming more accessible, so I encourage you to look into replacing single-life plastic with compostable dishes and silverware.

Served on a 20" (51 cm) board

1 serving Luscious Chocolate Pudding, or 4 cups (200 g) instant

8 x 1 oz (28 g) snack bags of OREO cookies, ⅔ of the cookies crushed, ⅓ left whole to garnish

3 bananas, sliced

3 kiwis, peeled and sliced

2 cups (340 g) strawberries, sliced

2 cups (290 g) blueberries

1 cup (161 g) maraschino cherries

⅓ cup (58 g) sprinkles

canned whipped cream

NOTES

- Use instant chocolate pudding in a pinch.
- Toss the bananas in lemon juice to prevent browning.
- It's essential to cut the tops of the bags off, but do not pull open, or they will tear down the sides and not be usable.
- Use any kind of cookie snack bags you'd like; chocolate chips, vanilla wafers, and Nutter Butters would also be delicious!
- I love the richness that egg yolks lend to pudding, but if you'd like to only use cornstarch, replace the egg yolks with 2½ tablespoons (20 g) more cornstarch.
- This pudding can be served warm or chilled.
- You can also use recipe in trifles, parfaits, pies, and more.
- When mixing the chocolate into the pudding, make sure to not add any water or else the chocolate might seize.

Chocolate Pudding

Makes about 4 cups | Prep time: 10 minutes | Cook time: 15–20 minutes, plus 4-hour chill time

3 cup (705 ml) whole milk, divided

3 tablespoons (24 g) cornstarch

½ cup (120 ml) heavy cream

¾ cup (150 g) white sugar

2 pinches of kosher salt

3 tablespoons (16 g) cocoa powder

½ teaspoon espresso or instant coffee powder (optional)

3 large egg yolks

2 oz (55 g) 60 percent cocoa chocolate, finely chopped

3 tablespoons (42 g) butter, cubed

1. In a small mixing bowl, whisk together ¼ cup (60 ml) cold milk and cornstarch until smooth, with no visible lumps. Set aside.

2. In a medium pot, whisk together the remaining milk, cream, sugar, salt, cocoa powder, and espresso powder. Bring the heat to medium-low and stir until steam comes off the top and the sugar dissolves, about 4 minutes.

3. Add the egg yolks to a medium bowl, then slowly, while whisking vigorously, pour in half of the hot milk, until the eggs are tempered. Stir the tempered yolks back into the pot, along with the cornstarch mixture— if desired, use a fine-mesh sieve to ensure there are no lumps. Stir constantly until the pudding is viscous enough to thickly coat the back of a spoon, but not so thick that it looks gelatinized; 10–12 minutes.

4. Immediately remove from heat and let sit for 4–5 minutes to cool slightly, then stir in the chopped chocolate just until dispersed, not melted. Let sit for 30–60 seconds to allow the pieces to melt in the residual heat. Once melted, add the butter and stir until smooth. Transfer to a bowl and refrigerate until chilled and set, at least 4 hours. To prevent a skin from forming, lightly grease a sheet of plastic and place it directly on the pudding's surface.

Campfire S'Mores Cookie Dough Fondue

If I had developed this recipe years ago, I know that my kids would have lost their minds with excitement at the thought of dipping cookies, berries, nuts, and graham crackers into a molten mix of peanut butter, cookie dough, chocolate, and marshmallows with a scoop of vanilla ice cream on the side. This recipe is every child's—*and* adult's—campfire dessert dream. The recipe is obviously not very technical, the ingredients simply need to melt together at a high enough temperature to liquify into salty sweet lava. However, if you're making this over a campfire the cook time will likely vary depending on the heat of the flames, so keep an eye on it as it cooks.

Serves 8–10 | Prep time: 5–10 minutes | Cook time: 25 minutes

2 tablespoons (28 g) butter

16 jumbo marshmallows

7 tablespoons (112 g) chunky peanut butter

8 oz (225 g) safe-to-eat raw cookie dough (sugar cookie flavor)

4 oz (115 g) bittersweet Baker's chocolate, broken into squares

Sea salt to taste (optional)

FOR THE BOARD

12 large strawberries

2 cups (250 g) raspberries

7 oz (198 g) graham crackers

5 oz (140 g) OREO cookies (thins)

½ cup (55 g) toasted pecans, chopped

2 cups (240 g) mini pretzels

6 oz (170 g) strawberry thumbprint cookies

4–6 single servings ice cream

1. In a 10" (25 cm) cast-iron skillet, add the butter, followed by a layer of marshmallows. Dollop on the peanut butter and cookie dough, then place the chocolate squares on top.

2. If you're making this over a fire, cover the top with parchment (making sure none of it hangs over the edges and can catch on fire), and then cover tightly with foil and cook for 20–25 minutes over medium heat.

3. If cooking in an oven, bake at 400°F (200°C, or gas mark 6) for 12–15 minutes covered, until the marshmallows are melted and gooey. Remove the foil and cook for an additional 10 minutes, until lightly golden.

4. Cool for 10 minutes before setting on the board or serving. If desired, sprinkle the fondue with a pinch of sea salt.

5. Prepare the board with a hot pad for the hot skillet. Arrange the other foods and add the skillet last.

6. Dip and enjoy!

PART 2

FALL/ WINTER

> "It looked like the world was covered in a cobbler crust of brown sugar and cinnamon."
>
> **—Sarah Addison Allen**

It's hard to let go of summer, but what makes the goodbye a little easier for me is how the grocery stores begin to carry my favorite autumn produce. It's a season to slow down, migrate more to the cozy indoors, and take some deep, cleansing breaths.

Here in the high desert of central Oregon, we sometimes get to experience all four seasons in one short day this time of year—rain, snow, warmth, and cold. We joke about it on the street, on the bike paths, and over warm cups of coffee.

Each season has its novelties. In the fall, it's a celebration of the senses: crisp breezes, even crisper apples, golden light, and painted trees.

It's also the season to buy late-summer berries from our farmers' markets (or pick them yourself) and make a pie or cobbler board, to gift to the neighbors. Or invite them over—a lovely way to end the summer and begin the fall together.

My mom used to do this as a simple farm girl in Phoenix, Oregon. She blessed her neighbors with out-of-this-world homemade fruit and cream pies. She taught me how to make them, and more importantly, why it's so fulfilling to give them away.

So let's allow colorful fall—and her more serene sister, winter, whose snow makes all things dimly beautiful—redirect our passions from carefree days of summer to our homier loves like cooking, baking, and gathering around the fire. It's a great time for soups, sauces, braised meat, and freezing what you don't eat—only to discover these frozen delights months later, as we melt into spring.

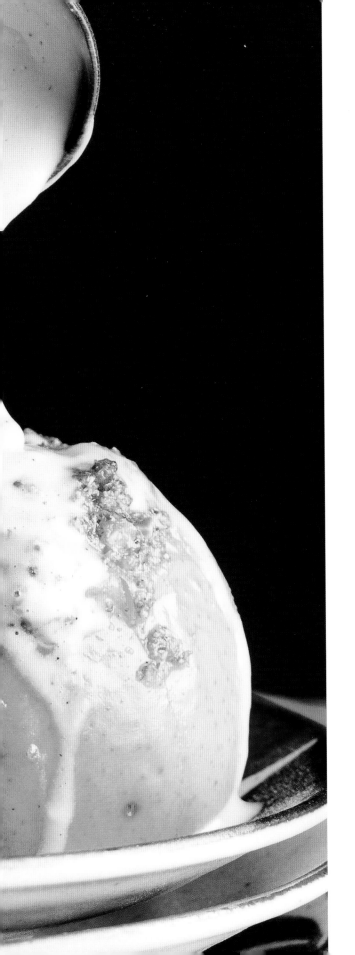

CHAPTER 4

Keeping it Small: Recipes for 2 to 4

Roasted Apple Crispy Prosciutto Crostini

Apples are something that I always have in my fruit bowl—they're delicious as a snack, on salads, in desserts, and perfect for a light appetizer. With these crostini, all you need are a few delicious bites, paired with your favorite wine, to get ready for the next course!

Serves 12 | Prep time: 20 minutes | Cook time: 25–30 minutes

1 medium-large Honeycrisp apple, sliced ½" (1 cm) thick

1½ tablespoons (30 g) honey

¾ teaspoon fresh black pepper

½ teaspoon kosher salt

1½ tablespoons (5 g) rosemary, finely chopped

2 tablespoons (28 g) unsalted butter, cubed

10 x 1" (2.5 cm)-thick strips of prosciutto

⅓ cup (40 g) Gorgonzola cheese, crumbled

12 slices French bread cut ¾–1" (2–2.5 cm) thick, toasted with oil

ROAST THE APPLES

1. Preheat the oven to 400°F (200°C, or gas mark 6).

2. Line a small baking dish or baking tray with parchment paper.

3. Toss the sliced apples in a medium bowl with the honey, pepper, salt, and rosemary, and spread onto the sheet. Sprinkle the butter cubes on top.

4. Bake on the center rack for 18–20 minutes until softened, tossing halfway through. Once the apples are fragrant and golden, remove from the oven and set aside to cool.

PREPARE THE PROSCIUTTO

5. On a lightly greased baking sheet, arrange the prosciutto into 2" (5 cm)-long bundles. Gently wrap the prosciutto around two fingers like a ribbon, to give dimension and folds as they crisp up in the oven, then carefully slide them off, keeping the shape. Place the prosciutto one rack below the broiler, and broil on a low setting for 4–5 minutes or until darkened in color, sizzling, and crisp. Remove from the oven.

6. Layer the apple, prosciutto, and Gorgonzola cheese crumbles on top of sliced French bread. Serve warm immediately.

Curry Sweet Potato Soup with Herbed Meatballs

This silky soup and tender meatball combo packs a lot of flavor into every single bite! Inspired by the flavors of Indian cuisine, the soup will taste better the longer it sits, so it is ideal for weekday meal prep. Both the cooked soup and meatballs can be frozen for up to three months and reserved for a last-minute meal. Best of all, they can be used as separate recipes or even made into boards. The meatballs can be served with grains, broths, pasta, or lettuce cups, and the soup can be served over rice with steamed vegetables, tofu, chickpeas, and other proteins.

Herbed Turkey Meatballs

Makes 12–15 meatballs | Prep time: 15 minutes | Cook time: 35 minutes

1½ teaspoons smoked paprika

1½ teaspoons coriander

1 teaspoon black pepper

¼ teaspoon ground cardamom

½ teaspoon kosher salt

2 teaspoons dark soy sauce (or 1 tablespoon [15 ml] regular)

2 teaspoons brown sugar

1 lb. (455 g) ground turkey

½ cup (8 g) cilantro, finely chopped

¼ cup (26 g) green onion, chopped

⅓ cup (27 g) crumbled Parmesan

1 small egg, beaten

2 tablespoons (28 g) ghee (clarified butter)

1. In a small mixing bowl, combine the paprika, coriander, pepper, cardamom, and salt. In a small, separate bowl, combine the soy sauce and brown sugar, mixing until mostly dissolved, approximately 2 minutes. Set aside.

2. In a wide mixing bowl, spread the meat into a single layer to provide even seasoning and reduce the chance of overmixing. Sprinkle with the dry seasonings, cilantro, green onion, Parmesan, and soy sauce/brown sugar mixture. Add the egg, then using a spoon or your hands, gently mix together until just combined. Don't over-mix, as this will lead to an unpleasant texture. Portion into twelve to fifteen meatballs, about 3 tablespoons (45 g) each, and place on a parchment-lined plate.

3. In a large skillet, or working in batches, heat the ghee over medium-high heat. Add the meatballs into the pan in a clockwise fashion; this helps to keep track of which one to flip first. Cook each side for 10–12 minutes before removing from the pan; flip when the meatballs are cooked a little more than halfway through. If the bottoms are browning too quickly, reduce the heat to medium or medium-low. If needed, insert a thermometer into the center and cook until it reaches 165°F (75°C). Remove from the pan, cover with foil, and allow to rest.

Curry Sweet Potato Soup

Serves 4 | Prep time: 25 minutes | Cook time: 45 minutes

1 small yellow onion, diced

3 cloves garlic, crushed

2 tablespoons (28 g) ghee

1 jalapeño or serrano chili, diced

1½ teaspoons kosher salt, plus more to taste

1½ tablespoons (10 g) curry powder

1 teaspoon ground cumin

½ teaspoon cayenne

¾ teaspoon smoked paprika

¾ teaspoon fresh black pepper

1 large roasted sweet potato (1½ cups [165 g])

1½ tablespoons (25 ml) fish sauce

1 teaspoon dark soy sauce (2 teaspoons regular soy sauce)

1 x 14-oz (425 ml) can full-fat coconut milk

2 cups (475 ml) chicken stock

1. In the same pan that the meatballs were cooked in, sauté the onions and garlic; use a paper towel to remove any black, burnt bits in the pan, then heat 2 tablespoons (28 g) ghee over medium heat. Add the onion, garlic, jalapeño, and a pinch of salt. Reduce the heat to medium-low and cook until softened, 8–10 minutes. Add the curry powder, cumin, cayenne, paprika, and pepper and cook until fragrant, 90 seconds.

2. Add the sweet potato, fish sauce, soy sauce, coconut milk, and chicken stock. Stir to combine. Reduce over medium-low heat for 8–10 minutes. Taste for salt, then transfer to a blender, or use a hand blender, and purée until smooth. Taste for additional seasoning.

3. Add the meatballs to the soup and serve.

NOTES

- Wet your hands before rolling the meatballs to prevent sticking. Additionally, to check that the seasoning is right before you portion and roll out the meatballs, cook a little meat to make sure the flavors are balanced.

- When cooking the meatballs, try to use a large pan, or two pans, so you can cook all of them at once.

- A day or two before making the soup, roast the sweet potato at 400°F (200°C, or gas mark 6) for 60–75 minutes depending on the size. Poke the skin with a fork before putting in the oven.

- Use tamari soy sauce for a gluten-free alternative.

Braised Tomato and Olive Chicken

Braised dishes are some of my favorites to make because they're impressively flavorful but don't require hours of preparation. They also make for the best leftovers, because the longer the dish sits, the deeper the flavor becomes. In this recipe, chicken is cooked slowly in warm, jammy, spiced tomatoes with sweet pops of plump raisin, briny caper pearls, and sharp olives. Braising with skin-on, bone-in chicken pieces is important, because both lend flavor to the dish. Creamy crumbled feta cheese, fresh herbs, and more marinated olives marry the tomato and chicken flavors deliciously. Goat cheese, Parmesan, and cilantro would be complimentary as well.

Serves 4 | Prep time: 40 minutes | Cook time: 2–2½ hours

OLIVE CHICKEN

1 skin-on, bone-in chicken, divided into 2 drumsticks, 2 thighs, and 2 breasts

kosher salt to season chicken and to taste

2 teaspoons fresh black pepper, plus more to season chicken

6 tablespoons (90 ml) olive oil, divided

2 teaspoons sweet paprika

½ teaspoon cayenne pepper

2 teaspoons ground cumin

½ teaspoon ground allspice

6 cloves garlic, crushed

1 small yellow onion, cut into ¼" (6 mm) half moons

1 tablespoon (16 g) tomato paste

1 cup (235 ml) white wine

1 x 14-oz (400 g) can crushed tomatoes

⅔ cup (100 g) golden raisins

12 oz (340 g) pitted green and Kalamata olive medley, divided

3 tablespoons (26 g) capers

2 bay leaves

⅓ cup (75 g) crumbled feta to serve

fresh parsley and mint, chopped

1. Preheat the oven to 275°F (140°C, or gas mark 1).

2. Rinse and pat dry the chicken parts. Generously season the front and back of each with salt and black pepper. Allow the chicken to rest for at least 30 minutes before cooking. You can season the chicken up to 2 days prior to serving.

3. Once the chicken has marinated, pat dry once more. Add 3 tablespoons (45 ml) of olive oil to a 4.5 qt. (4.3 L) braiser, or similar-sized vessel, over medium-high heat. When the oil is hot and shimmery, lay the chicken pieces in, skin side down. Sear for 2–3 minutes, then the reduce heat to medium and cook for 4–5 minutes more, until brown and crisp. Flip the pieces, cook for 5 minutes, then remove from the pan, and set aside.

4. Add the remaining olive oil to the pan. Once hot, add the sweet paprika, cayenne, cumin, allspice, and 2 teaspoons black pepper. Stir frequently until fragrant, about 90 seconds. Add the garlic, onions, tomato paste, and a pinch of salt; reduce the heat to medium. Salt to taste and cook for 8–10 minutes until translucent. Pour in the white wine, scraping the bottom with a spoon to deglaze. Bring the wine to a simmer and cook until reduced by half, about 3 minutes. Once reduced, add the crushed tomatoes, and increase the heat to bring to a boil, then reduce the heat, and simmer for 8 minutes. Sir in the raisins,

(continued)

FOR THE BOARD

crunchy baguette, basmati rice, or couscous

side of steamed or roasted veggies

sliced apples or oranges

side salad of baby greens, cucumber, tomato, red onion, chickpeas, toasted almonds, lemon vinaigrette

a dessert like baklava or honey-sweetened ricotta with peaches and almonds

FOR GARNISHES

herbs

olives

cheeses

plain, whole-fat yogurt

sour cream

8 ounces (225 g) of olives, capers, and bay leaves, and season with about 2 teaspoons of kosher salt. Nestle the chicken pieces into the liquid, but do not submerge.

5. Cover with a lid and place on the center rack of the oven for 70 minutes. Remove the lid and continue cooking for 45 minutes more, or until meat has reached 165°F (75°C) and the sauce has reduced to a jammy consistency. If needed, the sauce can be reduced on the stovetop after the chicken is done.

6. Remove from the oven and allow to cool 15–20 minutes before garnishing with feta, herbs, and remaining olives.

Cheesy Lasagna Boats

Lasagna boats are a festive fall alternative to traditional lasagna. If you're looking for a vegetarian, dairy-free option, swap the ground meat for chopped mushrooms and the cheeses for their vegan alternatives. If you're just making this for two people, halve the ingredients for the ricotta filling and the Simple Red Sauce. If you make a full batch of red sauce and don't use it all, store in the freezer for up to 3 months. To make a board from these boats, serve them with a delicious garden salad, dressing, and sliced baguette.

Prep time: 25 minutes | Cook time: 1 hour 30–50 minutes

LASAGNA BOATS

2 spaghetti squash, seeded

1 tablespoon (15 ml) olive oil

salt and pepper to taste

SPINACH RICOTTA FILLING

8 oz (225 g) ricotta

1 lb. (455 g) frozen spinach, thawed and drained

¼ cup (10 g) basil, chiffonnade

½ teaspoon orange or lemon zest (optional)

1½ teaspoons kosher salt, plus more to taste

1½ teaspoons fresh cracked pepper

4 oz (115 g) shredded provolone; can substitute mozzarella or Parmesan cheese

1. Preheat the oven to 400°F (200°C, or gas mark 6). Drizzle the inside of each squash half with olive oil, salt, and pepper. On a parchment-lined sheet tray, arrange the squash, cut side down. Using a knife, prick the outer shell (to prevent unwanted squash explosions). Bake for 45–60 minutes (depending on the size), or until softened, with browning around the edges.

2. While the squash cooks, make the red sauce (see recipe on next page.) As the red sauce reduces, make the ricotta filling. In a medium mixing bowl, combine the ricotta, spinach, basil, zest, salt, pepper, and provolone. Taste for salt and set aside.

3. Once the squash has cooked, allow to cool for 10–15 minutes, then use a fork to scoop the inside out into a medium mixing bowl. Season well with salt and pepper to taste; set aside.

4. In the empty shells, layer ricotta, red sauce, squash, and a generous pinch of cheese (reserving 2 cups [230 g] for the tops); repeat once more until shells are nearly full. Top with the remaining cheese and return to the oven for 45–50 minutes more until the tops and edges have browned. If you like a denser, dryer lasagna, add 5–10 more minutes.

5. Let cool 10–15 minutes before serving.

Simple Red Sauce

Prep time: 15 minutes | Cook time: 1 hour 20 minutes

¼ cup (59 ml) olive oil, plus more if needed

1 lb. (455 g) ground pork; can substitute chicken, beef, or chopped cremini mushrooms

1½ teaspoons kosher salt, plus more to taste

2 teaspoons fresh black pepper

1 teaspoon crushed fennel seeds (optional)

2 tablespoons (17 g) Italian seasoning, divided

1 small yellow onion, diced

4 cloves garlic, crushed

2 teaspoons Calabrian chili paste (optional)

1½ tablespoons (24 g) tomato paste

1 x 28 oz (800 g) can crushed tomatoes

½ cup (120 ml) chicken stock

1. In a large pot over medium-high heat, add the olive oil. Once shimmery, add the ground meat and sprinkle with 1½ teaspoons salt, pepper, and fennel seeds. Let sit, untouched, for 5–6 minutes to brown, then stir in 1 tablespoon (8.5 g) of Italian seasoning. Once browned, use a slotted spoon to remove the meat, leaving behind any oil or rendered fat. Set the meat aside.

2. Reduce the heat to medium—adding a drizzle of oil if there isn't much left behind—and add the onion and garlic to the pot. Reduce the heat to medium-low; season with salt and cook until translucent, 8–10 minutes. Once softened, increase the heat to medium-high and add in the chili paste, Italian seasoning, tomato paste, and salt and pepper to taste. Cook until the pastes caramelize and deepen in color, about 2 minutes. Add the crushed tomatoes, chicken stock, and ground meat. Bring to a boil, then reduce the heat to simmer. Reduce the sauce for 45–60 minutes until thickened and flavorful; salt to taste toward the end of reducing so as to not oversalt.

Chicken Tikka Masala Pizza

Don't get me wrong, basic cheese pizza is great, but the Indian version takes a classic to a new level. India's rich array of spices and piquant flavors can transform a mundane weeknight meal into an exciting sensory adventure. Additional dips and sauces to serve with the pizza include tamarind honey, listed below, as well as mint and mango chutneys. While this recipe is not traditional, consider it as an opportunity to learn more about Indian food and other ways you can spice up standard American fare.

Serves 4 | Prep time: 50 minutes, including time for pizza sauce;
excludes time for chicken tenders | Cook time: 12–15 minutes

PIZZA

¼ recipe Chicken Tikka Masala Tenders (page 167)

½ recipe Tikka Masala Pizza Sauce, recipe (page 143)

cornmeal for dusting

1 lb. (455 g) store-bought pizza dough

TOPPINGS

¼ recipe Chicken Tikka Masala Tenders

½ cup (40 g) Parmesan, shredded or crumbled

¾ cup (86 g) low-moisture mozzarella cheese, shredded

½ cup (75 g) feta, crumbled

½ cup (45 g) purple cabbage, thinly shaven

TAMARIND HONEY

1 tablespoon (15 g) tamarind paste

1½ tablespoons (30 g) honey

MARINATE THE CHICKEN

1. One to two days in advance, marinate the Chicken Tikka Masala Tenders (see page 167). Before cooking the pizza, broil the tenders according to the recipe. Additionally, combine the tamarind and honey and set aside until ready to serve.

ASSEMBLE AND COOK THE PIZZA

1. Preheat the oven to the highest temperature possible and place a pizza stone on the bottom rack. Allow at least 30 minutes for the stone to heat at full temperature before assembling the pizza. Let the dough, store-bought or homemade, sit out for 30 minutes or so before cooking.

2. Spread cornmeal onto a clean, large workspace. Using your hands, stretch the dough into a 13–15" (33–38 cm) circle, being careful not to stretch it too thin and tear. Place onto the cornmeal so it can be lifted off the counter when you're ready to assemble.

3. Before you're ready to bake your pizza, remove the pizza stone from the oven and place on a heat-proof surface.

4. Transfer the pizza dough to the hot stone. Working quickly, spread ¾–1 cup (175–235 ml) of sauce into a single layer, followed by half of the Parmesan and mozzarella, the chicken, and purple cabbage. Top with the remaining cheeses and return to the lower center rack of the oven for 12–15 minutes, or until the cheese is golden and bubbling.

5. Let cool for 10–15 minutes, cut into slices, and serve with the tamarind honey.

Tikka Masala Pizza Sauce

Makes 2 cups (475 ml) | Prep time: 15 minutes | Cook time: 45 minutes

4 tablespoons (55 g) ghee

1 teaspoon sweet paprika

1 teaspoon coriander

¼ teaspoon turmeric

½ teaspoon black pepper

½ teaspoon Kashmiri chili powder, or other chili powder

2 tablespoons (13.4 g) garam masala

1 small yellow onion, diced

1 green chili, diced

1½ tablespoons (15 g) minced garlic

1 tablespoon (6 g) minced ginger

1½ teaspoons salt, plus more to taste

1 x 14-oz (400 g) can crushed tomatoes

¼ cup (60 ml) water

1 tablespoon (20 g) honey

3 tablespoons (45 ml) heavy cream

1. In a medium skillet, heat 3 tablespoons (42 g) of ghee over medium-high heat. Once shimmery and hot, bloom the spices (see notes) and stir for 30 seconds until fragrant, then add the remaining ghee, onions, chili, garlic, ginger, and salt. Reduce the heat to medium-low and cook until the onions and chilis are softened, 12 minutes.

2. Add the tomatoes, water, honey, and heavy cream, bring to a simmer, and reduce until thickened, 30–35 minutes, stirring semi-frequently. If you prefer, use an emulsion blender to purée some of the sauce for a slightly smoother consistency. This sauce can also be made up to four days in advance.

NOTES

- Blooming spices is the process of frying ground spices in fat, and is a secret weapon technique found in many cultures that is used to intensify the flavor of the sauce.

- The pizza sauce is essentially a thicker tikka masala pizza sauce, this ensures it doesn't leave excess moisture on the pizza. The recipe for one pizza calls for about half of the yielded sauce, but I recommend making the whole recipe and freezing it, up to 3 months, for later use—if you're going to take the time to make it, you might as well get multiple meals out of it!

- Both the Tikka Masala Tenders and the pizza sauce are also used to make Tikka Masala Tender Bowls on page 165, just follow the directions on how to adapt the sauce for the bowls.

Miso Parmesan Udon Noodles

In this Japanese-Italian fusion dish, chewy, dense udon noodles are slathered in a glossy coconut sauce packed with umami flavor from shiitake mushrooms, white miso, and Parmesan. If you're not fond of coconut milk, swap it out for heavy cream. Additionally, the spinach can be substituted with another wilt-friendly variety. Either way, the end result is saucy, slurpable noodles that you won't be able to stop eating.

Serves 2–4 | Prep time: 10 minutes | Cook time: 20 minutes

3 tablespoons (45 ml) neutral oil

12 oz (340 g) shiitake mushrooms, stemmed, caps sliced ¼" (6 mm) thick

salt to taste

1 teaspoon soy sauce

1 teaspoon white pepper

3 cloves garlic, crushed

2 tablespoons (30 ml) white miso

2 teaspoons all-purpose flour

1 x 14-oz (425 ml) can full-fat coconut milk (substitute 1⅔ cups [395 ml] heavy cream)

1½ teaspoons honey

½ cup (50 g) Parmesan cheese, grated

4 cups (120 g) spinach

16 oz (455 g) udon noodles, fresh or frozen

⅓ cup (34.7 g) green onion, finely chopped

1 red Fresno chili, or other chili thinly sliced

1. In a medium skillet over medium-high heat, add 2 tablespoons (30 ml) oil. Once hot, add the mushrooms, a pinch of salt, soy sauce, and white pepper. Cook for 3–4 minutes until softened and browned. Add the remaining oil, garlic, and miso and reduce the heat to medium-low. Cook for 4 minutes until softened. Add the flour, cooking for 2 minutes, then stir in the coconut milk and bring to a boil; reduce the heat to medium-low and simmer 5 minutes more to thicken.

2. Once thickened, remove from the heat and stir in Parmesan and spinach leaves; cover with a lid and allow the spinach to wilt while you cook the noodles.

3. Cook the noodles according to package directions. Once cooked al dente, reserve ½ cup (120 ml) of pasta water, drain and return pasta back to the pot, along with the reserve water and coconut-miso sauce. Stir until the sauce is glossy and thickened.

4. Garnish with green onion and chili peppers and serve warm.

Date Goat Cheese Cookie Bars

Goat cheese is not an ingredient you encounter much outside of savory contexts like a salad, charcuterie board, or pizza. However, like sour cream, the cheese's dense, creamy, and tangy flavors work wonderfully in dessert form. These cookie bars have a crunchy cinnamon sugar crust, chewy pockets of chopped dates, and a subtle, tangy bite that—for me at least—is refreshingly addictive.

Serves 8

1 cup (225 g) unsalted butter, cubed ½" (1 cm) thick, plus 1–2 tablespoons (14–28 g) softened butter to grease pan

1½ tablespoons (19.5 g) white sugar

2 teaspoons ground cinnamon, divided

2 cups (250 g) and 3 tablespoons (23 g) all-purpose flour

1¼ cups (150 g) powdered sugar

1¼ teaspoons kosher salt

6 oz (168 g) goat cheese, crumbled and chilled

¾ cup (134 g) dates, pitted, chopped into small, ¼" (6 mm) pieces

½ heaping cup (55 g) chopped salted, toasted pecans

2 teaspoons vanilla extract

honey

flake salt

vanilla ice cream (optional)

NOTES

- Freeze the butter and goat cheese for 15 minutes before making the bars.

- Cinnamon makes the edges look browner than they are, so don't pull the pan out *too* soon.

1. Preheat the oven to 325°F (170°C, or gas mark 3). Grease an 8" x 8" (20 x 20 cm) metal baking dish with softened butter. Mix the white sugar and ½ teaspoon (2.3 g) cinnamon together and sprinkle into the pan, tilting to coat the bottom and sides. Set aside.

2. In a food processor, pulse together the flour, powdered sugar, salt, and 1½ teaspoons cinnamon until combined. Next, add in the butter and goat cheese; pulse, about 10–12 times, until cut into pea-size pieces, but still a dry, loose texture. Add the dates and pecans, using a spoon or your fingers to coat the pieces in flour to prevent clumping. Pour in the vanilla and pulse just until the dough has a fine texture, and holds together when pressed in your hand, but crumbles apart easily like fine, damp sand.

3. Pour into the greased baking dish and use the bottom of a measuring cup to press down into a flat, compact layer. Use a knife or fork to poke holes down to the base—use your fingers on each side of the blade to press the dough down and prevent it from breaking apart when you pull the utensil up. Bake on the center rack of the oven for 35–45 minutes, until just golden brown around the edges and dry.

4. Just as it comes out of the oven, use a sharp knife to cut into 8 bars and let cool on a rack completely before removing from the pan. To serve, drizzle with honey, flake salt, and if needed (and I think it is!) a scoop of vanilla ice cream.

Pear Puff Pastry Tart

A sheet of puff pastry has endless applications. It can be used for brunch, appetizers, main dishes, and—my favorite—desserts. I always try to keep a sheet of puff pastry in the freezer, especially during winter months when apples and pears are abundant. This spiced tart offers an ideal textural contrast between the crunchy, buttery, puff pastry dough, the softened, spiced pear, and velvety vanilla ice cream.

Serves 6 | Prep time: 5 minutes | Cook time: 32–35 minutes

1 sheet puff pastry, thawed

all-purpose flour for dusting

1 ripe Anjou pear, or other crisp variety like Forelle or Concorde

1 egg

3 tablespoons (42 g) butter

¾ teaspoon ground cinnamon

½ teaspoon ground cardamom

¼ teaspoon ground ginger

2 tablespoons (40 g) honey

¼ teaspoon salt

NOTE

- If you don't have a mandolin, quarter the pear into wedges, and thinly slice into smaller pieces.

1. Preheat the oven to 375°F (190°C, or gas mark 5). Line a rimmed baking sheet with parchment.

2. On a floured surface, roll out the puff pastry to an 11" x 13" (28 x 33 cm) rectangle, and transfer to the baking sheet.

3. Using a mandolin, carefully slice the pears lengthwise about 2 millimeters thin. Lay the pears onto the puff pastry, leaving a 1" (2.5 cm) border for the pastry to rise. Beat the egg with 1 teaspoon (5 ml) water and brush the entire tart with the egg wash. Bake for 17 minutes on the center rack.

4. In a small sauce pot, melt the butter over medium heat for 2 minutes. Stir in the spices, about 30 seconds, then add the honey and salt. Mix until dissolved for 2 minutes. Keep warm and set aside.

5. When the puff pastry is done, lower the oven temperature to 350°F (180°C, or gas mark 4). Remove the tart from the oven and drizzle with the spiced honey and butter mixture. Return to the oven for 15–18 minutes more, until golden.

6. Serve warm with Salted Brown Sugar Ice Cream (page 48).

Streusel Baked Apples with Vanilla Crème Anglaise

Crumbles, crisps, and stuffed apples have a few things in common: they all require a sweet, buttery topping to contrast with the tartness of the apple. These streusel-stuffed apples are a bit more tart than other baked apple desserts, and a bit more aesthetic as well. With an elegant touch of crème anglaise, the final dessert is balanced with just the right amount of tartness, sugar, and cream.

Prep time: 20 minutes | Cook time: 25–30 minutes

STREUSEL APPLES

4 mini-Honeycrisp, Fuji, Pink Lady, or Granny Smith apples

SPICED STREUSEL TOPPING

½ cup (48 g) and 2 tablespoons (12 g) almond flour

2 tablespoons (16 g) all-purpose flour

¼ cup (50 g) white sugar

2 tablespoons (60 g) brown sugar

¾ teaspoon ground cinnamon

½ teaspoon ground cardamom (optional)

pinch of allspice (optional)

⅓ cup (37 g) toasted hazelnuts or pecans

¼ teaspoon salt

6 tablespoons (85 g) butter, chilled and cubed

1 teaspoon vanilla extract

MAKE THE STREUSEL TOPPING

1. In a food processor, combine the almond flour, all-purpose flour, white sugar, brown sugar, cinnamon, cardamom, allspice, hazelnuts, and salt. Pulse until combined. Add the chilled butter pieces and vanilla, and pulse again until the topping is crumbly and just holds together when squeezed in your palm. Transfer to a bowl and freeze until ready to use.

2. Preheat the oven to 375°F (190°C, or gas mark 5) and line a rimmed baking sheet with parchment. Add 2 tablespoons (28 ml) of water into the pan to prevent burning.

CORE AND STUFF THE APPLES

3. Using a paring knife, gently prick the skin of the apple a few times, then, carefully insert the knife at an angle and cut a 1" (2.5 cm)-wide, cone-shaped opening around the apple stem. Using a small spoon, scoop out the core and seeds, creating a well for the streusel filling (making sure to leave the bottom intact). Once the apples are cored, pack them with 3–4 tablespoons (45–60 g) of filling, or until slightly overflowing from the top. Place on the baking sheet, and bake for 25–30 minutes, depending on the size of your apples. If you use larger apples, they will require more time, and a larger well in the center.

Crème Anglaise

Prep time: 5 minutes | Cook time: 10 minutes

3 small egg yolks

¾ cup (105 g) vanilla bean ice cream

2–3 tablespoons (28–45 ml) dark rum, bourbon, or 2 teaspoons rum extract

pinch of salt

1. While the apples bake, add the egg yolks to a small mixing bowl with a whisk, and set aside. Add the ice cream to a small sauce pot over medium heat, and melt until hot to the touch, but not scorched, about 2–3 minutes. Add a few tablespoons of the warmed ice cream to the egg yolks, whisking frequently so as not to cook the eggs. Once half of the warm ice cream is mixed in, add the tempered yolks back to the small sauce pot, along with the rum, over low heat. Stirring constantly, reducing the crème anglaise until it coats the back of a spoon, but is still fluid and pourable, about 3–5 minutes. Cover and keep warm until ready to serve.

2. Once the apples are done, allow them to cool a few minutes before serving. Cut the apples open and serve with a generous drizzle of warm crème anglaise.

NOTES

- The streusel topping makes 2 cups (250 g) because it's great to have some on hand in the freezer for future crumbles and crisps. If you don't want leftovers, halve the recipe.

- To make this gluten free, omit the flour and add 2 tablespoons (12 g) almond flour—the texture will be different, but the flavor will still be delicious.

- Keep an eye on the apples during the last 10 minutes of baking to make sure they don't begin to split open. If they do, take them out and let cool before serving.

CHAPTER 5

Feeding a Crowd: Recipes for Gathering

Winter Solstice Charcuterie Board

On this festive winter board, three seasonal appetizer recipes are included for inspiration—all of which are adaptable for seasonal produce. The Sausage, Sun-dried Tomato and Feta Toasts and the Bacon-wrapped Goat Cheese Stuffed Peppers satiate those winter cravings for dense, hearty appetizers, while the Pear Stilton Lettuce Cups offer a vegetarian, gluten-free alternative to heavy holiday appetizers.

Serves 8–10 | Made on a 26" (66 cm) Big Board

1 recipe Sausage, Sun-dried Tomato and Feta Toasts (page 156)

1 recipe Bacon-wrapped Goat Cheese Stuffed Peppers (page 157)

1 recipe Pear Stilton Lettuce Cups (page 156)

¼ lb. (115 g) brie

5 oz (140 g) Merlot BellaVitano cheese

½ lb. (225 g) Manchego cheese

5 oz (140 g) black truffle brie

2½ oz (125 g) Calabrese salami

2½ oz (125 g) prosciutto

butter crackers

Raincoast Crisps

crispbread crackers

2 blood oranges, quartered

1 lb. (455 g) green grapes

2 oz (55 g) pitted dried dates

6 oz (168 g) pitted mixed olives

1 Honeycrisp apple

1 raw artichoke heart to garnish

12 oz (340 g) pickled crunchy carrots

sparkling white wine

NOTE

- Keep extra appetizers warm in the oven, and refill the board as needed.

1. Prepare the board with the fresh ingredients, leaving room for the three appetizer recipes.

2. Serve with sparkling white wine!

Sausage Sun-dried Tomato and Feta Toasts

Makes 14–16 | Prep time: 15 minutes: | Cook time: 15–17 minutes

olive oil to drizzle

6 oz (168 g) baguette, cut into 14–16½" (36–42 cm)-wide, ¾" (2 cm)-thick slices

¼ cup (44 g) honey Dijon mustard

¼ cup (27.5 g) sun-dried tomatoes in oil

8 oz (225 g) feta cheese, cut into 14–16 pieces

1 lb. (455 g) raw sausage, casing removed, cut into 1½–2" (3.5–5 cm)-thick pieces

NOTES

- The sausage you use here should be greasy enough to render the fat onto the bread and crisp the bottom of it as it toasts in the oven.

- Goat or blue cheese would be a great substitute for feta.

1. Preheat the oven to 375°F (190°C, or gas mark 5). Line a rimmed baking sheet with parchment paper.

2. Drizzle the bread with olive oil, then spread about ½ teaspoon Dijon, followed by the sun-dried tomatoes, feta, and a piece of sausage on top. Skewer the bites with two toothpicks to keep them together and allow you to cut them in half after they're cold. Bake for 15 minutes, until the meat is fully cooked and the bottoms are crisp.

3. Let sit about 10 minutes after baking to cool, before cutting in half into smaller bites (if desired) and removing the skewers.

4. Serve immediately.

Pear Stilton Lettuce Cups

Serves 6–8 | Prep time: 10 minutes

1 large red Anjou pear, roughly chopped, skin on

1 teaspoon lemon juice

⅓ cup (37 g) toasted hazelnuts, roughly chopped

pinch of salt

½ cup (60 g) Stilton blue cheese crumbles

pomegranate seeds to garnish

1 small Belgian endive

1 baby butter leaf head

1 small radicchio head

1. In a medium bowl, add the chopped pear, lemon juice, hazelnuts, and a pinch of salt. Toss, then add the blue cheese crumbles. Transfer to a serving bowl and garnish with pomegranate.

2. Serve cold on endives, butter leaf, and radicchio.

NOTES

- Feel free to replace the pear with another winter fruit like apple or sliced grapes.

- You can also replace the cheese with something milder like feta or goat cheese, as well as the nuts with toasted walnuts or pecans.

Bacon-wrapped Goat Cheese Stuffed Peppers

Makes 12–15 bites | Prep time: 20 minutes | Cook time: 30–35 minutes

12 oz (340 g) whole roasted bell peppers, drained and patted dry

6 oz (168 g) goat cheese, softened

1 tablespoon (2.5 g) basil, minced

1 teaspoon fresh cracked black pepper

3 tablespoons (60 g) honey, plus more to garnish

8 slices thin-cut bacon, halved to make 16

NOTES

• If you don't have a wire rack, place the bites on the parchment. They won't be as crisp, but they will still be delicious. Just be sure to flip the bites 2–3 times.

• If you're using a wire rack, be sure to spray both sides with cooking spray to make for an easier clean up.

• It's important to use thinner bacon that can be stretched to fit around the pepper. If the bacon doesn't fit, use large, longer strips.

• Use the bacon to cover the exposed cheese, to prevent it from leaking from the sides. The peppers should look a bit square.

• Some jars of roasted bell peppers may come with irregular pepper sizes, so if you need to make more than 12, buy two jars to cover your bases.

1. Preheat the oven to 350°F (180°C, or gas mark 4). Line a rimmed baking sheet with parchment paper and set a well-greased wire rack on top (see notes).

2. Prepare the peppers: Using paper towels, let the peppers sit and dry for 5 minutes; you want them as dry as possible. Once drained, cut the peppers into two long strips about 1½" (3.5 cm) thick. Set aside on paper towels while you mix the cheese.

3. In a small bowl, mix together the softened cheese, basil, pepper, and honey. Spread about 1 tablespoon (15 g) tablespoons cheese mixture into the center of the bell pepper strip and roll up. Wrap the pepper, covering the open ends, with a slice of bacon. Secure with a toothpick and place on the wire rack.

4. Bake for 15 minutes, then increase the heat to 375°F (190°C, or gas mark 5), flip the bites, and bake for 15–20 minutes more until browned. If needed, flip once more and bake an additional 3–5 minutes.

5. Transfer to a paper towel-lined plate for a few minutes to cool, before serving with a drizzle of honey.

Roasted Grapes with Walnuts, Balsamic, and Yogurt

In this dish, creamy, plain yogurt accompanies rich balsamic vinegar, earthy winter savory, and tart roasted grapes to make a refreshing dish that leaves you wanting just one more bite. Serve as an appetizer alongside crunchy bread, crackers, and cured olives, or spoon it onto chicken or fish for a main dish.

Savory is an herb that originates near the Mediterranean, and there are two varieties: summer savory, a spicier, sweeter variety; and winter savory, an earthier, slightly bitter variety. Because this herb is not commonly found in most grocery stores, thyme, rosemary, or another hardy herb can take its place.

Serves 4–6 | Prep time: 10 minutes | Cook time: 15 minutes

1½ tablespoons (22.5 g) olive oil

1 shallot (about ⅓ cup [53 g]), thinly sliced with mandolin

2 teaspoons savory, rosemary, or thyme leaves, finely chopped

salt and pepper to taste

3 cups (450 g) red seedless grapes, halved

2 tablespoons (30 ml) balsamic vinegar

½ cup (60 g) toasted walnuts, chopped

plain whole-fat yogurt to serve (optional)

1. Preheat the oven to 450°F (230°C, or gas mark 8).

2. In a medium to large oven-safe skillet, heat the olive oil over medium-high heat, then add the shallots and chopped savory. Season with a pinch of salt and pepper; reduce the heat to medium and sauté for 4 minutes. Add the grapes and balsamic vinegar and transfer to the oven. Roast for 7 minutes, then remove from the oven and use a slotted spoon to remove the grapes and shallots, leaving the rendered juices behind in the pan. Combine the roasted grapes with the toasted walnuts, lightly season with salt, and set aside to cool, approximately 5 minutes.

3. On the stovetop, bring the liquids to a simmer, and reduce for 3–4 minutes until thickened. Spoon the yogurt onto a serving plate or bowl and top with the roasted grape mixture. Drizzle with the grape juice and balsamic reduction. This dish can be served warm or chilled.

Cacio e Pepe Mac and Cheese Bites

I love to serve these bites as an appetizer; they'll remind your guests of growing up but deliver an adult spin in the form of tangy Pecorino and lots of pepper. Because they can be prepped and baked up to 48 hours in advance, and rebaked before serving, they're an easy make-ahead appetizer; plus, double-baking leaves them extra crispy on the edges and can save you a bit of time. Both recipes feed a crowd, so if you don't need such a large batch, just halve the recipes!

If you prefer your mac and cheese straight from the stovetop, just dive in after the mornay sauce is added—or transfer it to a baking dish, sprinkle with panko, and bake in a 2-quart (1.9 L) dish at 350°F (180°C, or gas mark 4) until bubbling; about 15–17 minutes.

Makes 48 bites | Prep time: 15 minutes | Cook time: 55 minutes

---

2 heaping cups (240 g) Gruyère cheese, grated

6 tablespoons (85 g) butter, divided

½ cup (25 g) panko breadcrumbs

2 teaspoons salt

1½ tablespoons (9 g) fresh cracked pepper

3 tablespoons (23 g) all-purpose flour

4 cups (946 ml) whole milk

1 heaping cup (80 g) Pecorino Romano, crumpled or finely grated

1 lb. (455 g) mini shells, macaroni bows, or shell pasta, cooked

Calabrian Chili Marinara Sauce

MAKE THE PANKO CRUMBS

1. Preheat the oven to 375°F (190°C, or gas mark 5).

2. Grease two 24-cup mini muffin tins with nonstick spray. Evenly divide the Gruyère cheese into the bottom of each cup; set aside.

3. In a small skillet over medium heat, melt 2 table-spoons (28 g) of butter, then combine with the panko crumbs and salt to taste. Stir semi-frequently until golden brown; 3–4 minutes. Set aside.

MAKE THE MORNAY SAUCE

4. Over medium heat, add 4 tablespoons (55 g) butter and the pepper; cook until fragrant, 2–3 minutes. Whisk in the flour and cook out for 1–2 minutes, until foamy and darkened. Whisk in the milk and bring to a simmer. Cook for 7–10 minutes, until reduced by about two-thirds. Take the pan off the heat and whisk in the Pecorino until combined. Set aside.

COOK THE PASTA

5. Cook the pasta according to the package directions, making sure it remains al dente. When the pasta is almost done cooking, reserve ⅛ cup (28 ml) of the pasta water.

6. Quickly drain the pasta and immediately put it back into the pot. It's okay if some water remains after draining. Pour in the Mornay sauce. Stir until just thick enough to coat the back of a spoon, 4 minutes.

NOTES

- These can be made in larger muffin tins by simply adding 10–12 minutes more to the baking time, and a little more cheese to the bottom.

- To reheat the bites, bake at 375° (190°C, or gas mark 5) for 10–14 minutes until crisped.

- The Calabrian Chili Marinara Sauce also works as a pasta sauce—just use an immersion blender or a food processor to blend it smooth before stirring in some al dente noodles and Parmesan cheese.

- The marinara can also be served warm as an appetizer, with Cacio e Pepe Mac and Cheese bites, or, if you broil the top with shredded Italian cheeses, as a dip with prawns, warmed baguette pieces, or even roasted veggies.

MAKE THE MAC AND CHEESE BITES

7. Portion out the pasta into the muffin tins, about 2½ tablespoons (32 g) per tin. Top each with a pinch of panko crumbs. Bake for 10–15 minutes until crisp, brown, and bubbling along the edges, 25–30 minutes.

8. Remove from the oven and allow the bites to cool for 20–25 minutes. This allows them to solidify before removing from the tin.

9. Serve the bites warm, with Calabrian Chili Marinara Sauce to dip.

Calabrian Chili Marinara Sauce

Makes 4 cups (946 ml) | Prep time: 10 minutes | Cook time: 40 minutes

3 tablespoons (45 ml) olive oil

1 teaspoon fresh ground pepper

2 teaspoons Calabrian chili paste or chili flakes

1 tablespoon (16 g) tomato paste

1 small yellow onion, diced

3–4 cloves garlic, crushed or grated

salt to taste

3 tablespoons (45 ml) orange juice (optional)

1 x 28 oz (800 g) can whole, peeled tomatoes

3 basil stalks with leaves

1. In a medium sauce pot, add the olive oil over medium-high heat. Add the pepper, Calabrian chili paste, and tomato paste. Cook for 1–2 minutes, until fragrant and slightly darkened in color, then add the onion and garlic. Lower the heat to medium-low, season with salt, and cook until softened, 10 minutes.

2. Add the orange juice, tomatoes, and basil stalks. Bring to a boil, then reduce the heat and simmer for 30–40 minutes, until thickened. If desired, lightly purée half or all the sauce for a silkier texture.

3. Transfer the sauce to a dipping bowl and serve warm.

Monte Cristo Breakfast Casserole with Fried Sage

In this decadent—dare I say glutinous—recipe, Monte Cristo sandwiches are turned into a savory bread pudding. Bread stuffed with ham, mustard, and jam is soaked and baked in an eggy custard resulting in a tender, moist casserole that is ready to serve a crowd right when it comes out of the oven. The fried sage leaves are optional for a nice crunch and herbaceous note. If you do fry the sage leaves, save the frying oil for dressings, making eggs, or sautéing vegetables.

Prep: 15 minutes, plus 2–24 hours | Cook time: 45 minutes

MONTE CRISTO

⅓ cup (80 ml) heavy cream

1⅓ cups (315 ml) whole milk

5 large eggs

1¼ teaspoons kosher salt

1 teaspoon fresh ground pepper

1 lb. (455 g) white bread, sliced and stale

½ cup (160 g) raspberry rhubarb jam, or other red fruit jam

12 oz (340 g) Black Forest ham slices

¼ cup (44 g) honey mustard

6 oz (168 g) Swiss cheese, sliced

1¾ cups (210 g) shredded Gruyère cheese

⅓ cup (80 ml) olive oil

15 sage leaves

salt to season

NOTE

- Ideally, you'd use day-old, stale white bread to make this dish, but fresh bread will work as well. Just be careful not to compress it.

1. Prepare a 9" x 13" (23 x 33 cm) baking dish with cooking spray.

2. In a large bowl, whisk together the cream, milk, eggs, salt, and pepper. Set aside.

3. On a large surface, lay out the slices of bread into a single layer. On half the slices, spread about 1 tablespoon (20 g) of jam and arrange the ham on top. On the other slices, spread the honey mustard and top with Swiss cheese. Place the ham and Swiss cheese halves together and cut in half diagonally.

4. Place the triangles in the prepared pan, cut sides against the bottom. Slowly pour the custard over the sandwiches. Cover and chill overnight or at least 2 hours.

5. Preheat the oven to 350°F (180°C, or gas mark 4). Uncover the dish and sprinkle on the Gruyère cheese. Bake for 35–40 minutes, or until the cheese is golden and the eggs have set. If needed, broil the top for 2–3 minutes to brown the cheese further.

6. While the casserole bakes, fry the sage leaves. Line a sheet tray with paper towels and set out a slotted spoon. Heat the oil in a small to medium skillet over medium heat. When the oil is shimmery and hot, add the sage leaves in a single layer. When the leaves meet the oil, they will fizz and become fragrant. Allow each leaf to fry for 20–30 seconds until deepened in color, but not browned and burned—they will crisp up as they sit at room temperature. Use the slotted spoon to remove them onto the paper towels, and salt immediately. Allow to cool and crisp until ready to garnish.

7. Remove the casserole from the oven; let cool for 15 minutes before serving with fried sage leaves.

Tikka Masala Tender Bowls

This recipe is, of course, Indian-inspired; however, it is a bit more stripped down than the original, with various nontraditional elements and ingredients. The recipe calls for 2 pounds (907 g) total of protein because, if you're going to take the time to make the marinade and sauce, you might as well have leftovers for the week (leftovers that taste better the longer they sit, might I add). If you're looking for smaller portions and fewer leftovers, halve the recipe.

For a half-vegetarian option, swap in 1 pound (455 g) of paneer cheese for the second pound (455 g) of chicken. Marinate 1" (2.5 cm) paneer cubes in half of the yogurt marinade and add ¾ extra teaspoon of salt; let sit overnight, or up to three days. Cook in a large skillet over medium heat with 2 tablespoons (28 g) ghee, searing each side for 1 minute or so, covering with a lid in between each sear to soften the cheese.

Serves 6–8

THE BOARD

6–8 servings basmati rice, brown or white

chopped Persian or English cucumbers

fresh cilantro

mango chutney

Pickled Red Onions (page 43)

naan or other flat bread

NOTE

- If you're in an experimental mood, try adding aromatics, spices, dried fruit, and nuts to your rice for extra flavor and texture.

Tikka Masala Pizza Sauce (adapted)

Makes 3–4 cups (710–946 ml) | Prep time: 15 minutes | Cook time: 45 minutes

¾ cup (175 ml) water, total

⅓ cup (80 ml) heavy cream, total

⅓ cup (77 g) yogurt

salt to taste

1 cup (130g) frozen peas

1. Make the sauce according to the directions on page 143, but add the water, total heavy cream, yogurt to thin it out, additional salt to taste, and the frozen peas stirred in at the end until defrosted and warmed.

Chicken Tikka Masala Tenders

Serves 6–8 | Prep time: 20 minutes, plus 24-hour marinade time | Cook time: 10–15 minutes

2 lb. (907 g) chicken tenders or chicken thighs

4½ teaspoons (28.3 g) kosher salt, divided, plus more to taste

¼ cup (55 g) ghee

2 tablespoons (13.4 g) garam masala

1 tablespoon (7 g) ground cumin

1 teaspoon fresh ground pepper

2 teaspoons Kashmiri chili powder, or other chili powder

1 teaspoon fenugreek (optional)

¼ teaspoon cardamom

¾ cup (180 g) whole milk yogurt

1½ tablespoons (15 g) garlic, grated

2 tablespoons (40 g) honey or (60 g) brown sugar

1½ tablespoons (9 g) minced ginger

1. Make the marinade: Rinse, pat dry, and season both sides of the chicken tenders or thighs with about 2 teaspoons salt; transfer to a bowl. Cover each bowl and refrigerate.

2. In a small skillet or sauce pot, heat the ghee on medium-high. Once hot and shimmery, add the garam masala, cumin, black pepper, chili powder, fenugreek, and cardamom. Cook until fragrant, stirring frequently; 30–45 seconds. Transfer to a bowl and let cool for 5 minutes.

3. In a medium mixing bowl, combine the yogurt, remaining salt, garlic, honey, ginger, and the bloomed garam masala, cumin, black pepper, chili powder, cardamom, and fenugreek. Mix to combine, then add the chicken. Let marinate in the refrigerator overnight, or up to two days.

4. Before broiling the chicken, remove the tenders from the marinade, letting excess liquid drip off, and let it sit for 20 minutes at room temperature.

5. Preheat the broiler to high, and line a sheet tray with foil. Grease a wire rack well, making sure to spray the rack on both sides for easier clean up, and set on the foil. Arrange the chicken onto the rack, and place under the broiler, about 4–5 minutes each side, until slightly charred around the edges.

6. Once the chicken is cooked, set aside and let rest for 5 minutes before roughly chopping it. Stir it into the tikka masala pizza sauce with peas.

7. Serve warm over basmati rice with cucumbers, cilantro, chutney, Pickled Red Onions, and warm, toasted flatbread.

Miso Green Onion and Cheddar Biscuits

Biscuit dough is a blank canvas for all kinds of flavors. Cheese and herbs are a no-brainer for a savory spin, but miso is a less common addition. When miso is added to the mix, the dough is given a subtle, unexpected savoriness. In the oven the biscuits rise into a webbed, flaky stack of umami and aromatic deliciousness that can be dressed up as a decadent breakfast sandwich or eaten plain with a pat of melted butter. When making the dough, try to handle it lightly and as little as possible to yield tender, flaky biscuits.

Makes 6–8 biscuits | Prep time: 1 hour (includes 30-minute chill time) | Cook time: 20 minutes

1 egg

3 cups (375 g) all-purpose flour

1 tablespoon (13.8 g) baking powder

½ teaspoon baking soda

2 teaspoons white sugar

1 teaspoon kosher salt

2 tablespoons (32 g) miso, frozen for 30 minutes

12 tablespoons (170 g) butter, chilled and cut into pats

1 cup (112.5 g) cheddar cheese, shredded and frozen 30 minutes

¾ cup (34.7 g) green onion, minced

¾ cup (175 ml) buttermilk, chilled

1. In a small bowl, beat the egg with a splash of water; set aside.

2. In a large bowl, mix together the flour, baking powder, baking soda, sugar, and salt. Using your fingers, rub the miso into the flour until dispersed, then break the butter into pea-size pieces and roughly mix it into the dough. Once the butter is broken up, toss in the shredded cheese and green onion until dispersed. Create a well in the center and add half of the buttermilk; toss the dough upward using your fingers until the liquid is absorbed. Repeat for the remaining buttermilk; once the dough comes together into a shaggy ball (it's okay if there are still dry patches), turn it out onto a floured surface.

3. Using your hands or a rolling pin, roughly shape the dough into a 12" x 4" (30 x 10 cm) rectangle. Fold the outer edges to the center to create a trifold. Repeat this twice more, then finish by rolling into a 9" x 6" (23 x 15 cm) rectangle. Using a 3" (7.5 cm) ring, cut six biscuits. Gently combine and roll out the scraps to make one to two more biscuits, if possible.

4. Place on a parchment-lined plate or tray, one that will fit in your freezer. Let the biscuits chill 30 for minutes before baking.

5. While the biscuits chill, preheat the oven to 400°F (200°C, or gas mark 6).

6. Arrange the biscuits on a parchment-lined sheet tray and then brush the tops and sides with egg wash. Bake on the center rack for 20–22 minutes, until golden brown and risen. Let cool for 5 minutes before cutting in half.

Sweet and Savory Dutch Baby Board

Where I grew up, we called this dish a Hootenanny, which I think we can all agree is much more fun to say out loud than Dutch Baby. But by any name, this classic brunch recipe is foolproof. I add an egg yolk to make the final product extra custardy and eggy, as well as buttermilk for a subtle sharpness. On the board, sweet *and* savory toppings are included to satisfy everyone's taste.

Serves 4–6 | Prep time: 5 minutes | Cook time: 18–20 minutes | Made on a 20" (51 cm) board

NOTE

- Make sure the butter is hot before you pour the batter in, this helps it puff up.

DUTCH BABY

5 whole eggs

1 yolk

1 cup (235 ml) buttermilk

¾ cup (94 g) plus 2 tablespoons (16 g) all-purpose flour

¾ teaspoon salt

2 teaspoons white sugar

4 tablespoons (55 g) butter

THE BOARD

10–12 links breakfast sausage

1 Cara Cara orange, sliced

1 heaping cup (170 g) chopped strawberries

1 cup (145 g) blueberries

3 kiwis, sliced into half moons

1 small lemon, cut into wedges

⅓ cup (27 g) crumbled Parmesan cheese

⅓ cup (77 g) chive cream cheese

10–12 slices, cooked bacon

6 soft-boiled eggs, seasoned

⅓ cup (107 g) maple syrup

⅓ cup (27 g) toasted, sweetened coconut

1. Before baking the Dutch Baby, prepare your board with your desired savory and sweet toppings, sides, and drinks; additionally, place a hot pad where the Dutch Baby will be set.

2. Preheat the oven to 425°F (220°C, or gas mark 7). In a blender or bowl, whisk or blend the eggs, yolk, buttermilk, flour, salt, and sugar until combined.

3. Heat a large ovenproof skillet over medium-high; add the butter and melt until it is no longer foamy, about 2–3 minutes. Swirl the butter to coat the sides, then, while still very hot, pour in the batter, and immediately transfer to the oven and bake until puffed and golden, 18–20 minutes. Once cooked, immediately set on the board, and serve hot. Arrange other food items around the skillet for a beautiful breakfast board!

Deconstructed Waldorf Salad Board

This is a fresh, deconstructed salad that serves nicely on a board, with a bright, tangy dressing. It works beautifully in any season, as a side dish for any large meal or lunch spread, but it's especially nice for fall and winter when apples are crisp and crunchy. I love the versatility of large lettuce leaves—you can opt for lettuce wraps, a chopped salad in a bowl, or layering the ingredients in a glass parfait bowl. Let the party begin!

Serves 6–8 large portions | Prep time: 20 minutes | Made on a 26" (66 cm) Big Board

3 Persian cucumbers, sliced diagonally ¼" (6 mm) thick

1 cup (145 g) blueberries

16 oz ([455 g] about 3 cups) red and green grapes, halved

1 small Honeycrisp apple, sliced into ¼" (6 mm) half moons

1 small Granny Smith apple, sliced into ¼" (6 mm) half moons

1 cup (100 g) celery, cut into small, ¼" (6 mm) pieces

5 oz (140 g) bacon, cooked, roughly chopped

1 cup (110 g) toasted, salted pecans, roughly chopped

chopped mint, plus more sprigs to garnish

1. Lay the fruits and veggies in straight or curved lines, making sure to leave space for the bowls of chopped bacon and dressing. Place the bowls onto the board and garnish with small sprigs of mint and serve cold.

NOTES

- If in season, halved pitted cherries are also delightful on the board.
- You can prep the grapes, celery, bacon, and cucumber the night before. If prepping the apples, to keep them from turning brown, soak ahead in lemon juice. Because of the sourness of the lemon, you may need to add more honey to the dressing.

Dressing

Makes about 1 cup (235 ml)

⅓ cup (77 g) full-fat Greek yogurt

1½ tablespoons (22.5 ml) lime juice, plus zest of 1 lime

2 tablespoons (30 ml) olive oil

1 tablespoon (11 g) Dijon mustard

½ teaspoon honey

1 teaspoon kosher salt, plus more to taste

¾ teaspoon fresh cracked pepper

2 heaping tablespoon (8 g) parsley, finely chopped

2 tablespoons (12 g) mint, finely

1. In a small mixing bowl, combine the Greek yogurt, lime juice, zest, oil, mustard, honey, salt, pepper, parsley, and mint. Whisk until combined and creamy. Refrigerate until ready to use.

NOTE

- Substitute mayonnaise for Greek yogurt if that's your preference.

Caffe Mingo's Sugo di Carne

Years ago, my husband and I had dinner at Caffe Mingo, a tiny Italian restaurant in Portland, Oregon, with our dear friends, Lloyd and Laurel; everything about the night was memorable, especially the food. We asked the staff for their Sugo di Carne recipe, and they generously gave it to us. With a few small alterations over the years, it's still a favorite recipe to prepare ahead of time for company because the flavor intensifies the longer it sits.

Serves 12 | Prep time: 25 minutes | Cook time: 2½ hours

salt and pepper to season

1 5 lb. (2.3 kg) beef bottom round, cut into 2" (5 cm) cubes (beef top round roast is another option!)

2 tablespoons (30 ml) neutral, high-heat oil

14 tablespoons (198 g) butter

3 tablespoons (48 g) tomato paste

2 teaspoons brown sugar

3 red onions, halved, sliced about ¼" (6 mm) thick

1 x 750 ml bottle Chianti, or other fruity wine

1 x 28 oz (794 g) can whole peeled tomatoes with juice

1 cup (235 ml) brewed espresso

2 lb. (907 g) rigatoni or penne pasta

Parmesan cheese

fresh parsley, finely chopped

1. Preheat the oven to 400°F (200°C, or gas mark 6).

2. Season the beef generously with salt and pepper; cover and let sit for 30–45 minutes.

3. In a large Dutch oven, add 2 tablespoons (30 ml) neutral oil over medium-high heat. Once shimmery—working in batches and adding more neutral oil if needed—cook the beef until browned, about 5 minutes per batch, turning the pieces halfway through. Transfer the beef to a large bowl and set aside.

4. Reduce the heat to medium. Add the butter to the pot. Once melted, add the tomato paste and brown sugar and cook for 2 minutes, followed by the onions. Cook until softened, about 8 minutes.

5. Return the beef and juices to the pot. Add the wine, tomatoes with juice, and espresso. Bring to a boil, cover, and transfer to the oven.

6. Cook for 2–2½ hours and remove from the oven. Using a slotted spoon, transfer the beef to a bowl and let cool for 15 minutes. Using two forks, or your hands if the meat is cool enough to handle, shred the beef and set aside.

7. Using a blender or an immersion blender, purée the sauce until it is just emulsified—try to leave some texture in the sauce. Add the meat and sauce back into the pot and stir.

(continued)

NOTES

- I suggest you season the meat with salt and pepper at least 48 hours in advance for best results. Before browning, let the meat sit at room temperature for 30–45 minutes to come closer to room temperature.

- Making a dinner board out of this is simple, grab your Big Board and add a large basket of hot crunchy bread, a block of softened butter, a generous amount of shaven Parmesan cheese, a bowl of fresh chopped parsley, and a fresh garden salad.

8. Bring a large pot of water to a boil and season with salt. Once the water comes to a boil, add the pasta and cook until al dente. When there is about 2 minutes left for the pasta to cook, add ¾ cup (175 ml) of pasta water to the beef and stir.

9. Once cooked al dente, drain the pasta and add it to the beef. Stir until the sauce thickens and coats the noodles well. Also optional to keep separate, and let guests add their own pasta and meat sauce to their plate.

10. Serve warm, with Parmesan cheese and fresh chopped parsley. You can mix the pasta and sauce together (in a large pot) or serve separately. Serving separately gives the option to make several kinds of pasta (i.e., gluten-free, whole wheat), for a true "pasta bar."

11. On a small board, arrange hot bread in a basket with a plate of butter, and large shaved Parmesan, finely grated Parmesan, and chopped parsley to three small bowls. Serve on the side with the pasta dish.

Chinese-inspired Braised Beef

This is one of my family's favorite one-pot meals. I've been inspired by my daughter-in-law's Chinese cooking, which is the perfect balance of warm spices, sweetness, and umami. She's definitely upped the dinner game in our household! This recipe uses Chinese five spice, fresh minced ginger, and soy sauce. We also added Korean gochujang chili paste to the baby bok choy, for a little heat and depth of flavor.

Serves 4–6 | Prep time: 30 minutes | Cook time: 2½–3 hours

BRAISED BEEF

2.5 lb. (1.1 kg) Angus chuck roast

2½–3¾ teaspoons kosher salt, plus more to taste

3 large leeks, trimmed and washed

3 tablespoons (45 ml) neutral oil

⅓ cup (50 g) coconut sugar

1½ cups (255 ml) beef broth, warmed

⅓ cup (80 ml) soy sauce

3 large shallots, cut into large 1½" (3.5 cm) pieces

2 tablespoons (20 g) garlic, minced

2 tablespoons (12 g) ginger, minced

2 teaspoons ground cinnamon

1 teaspoon allspice

1 star anise

1 teaspoon white pepper (optional)

lime wedges

green onion

TO MAKE THE BRAISED BEEF

1. Prepare the meat 24–48 hours in advance with 1–1½ teaspoons kosher salt per pound. Cover and refrigerate until ready to braise. If you don't have time for this, simply salt the meat as soon as you can. Set the chuck out 20 minutes before searing.

2. Prepare the leeks; separate the top green section from the white. Cut the fibrous green pieces into 1" (2.5 cm) pieces. Cut the white bottoms into 2–2½" (5–6 cm) pieces. Set aside.

3. Preheat the oven to 325°F (170°C, or gas mark 3).

4. In a shallow braising dish, add the neutral oil and heat over medium-high heat. Once shimmery and hot, add the chuck, and sear 4 minutes each side until browned.

5. While the meat browns, combine the coconut sugar, warmed broth, and soy sauce. Stir to dissolve the sugar. Set aside.

6. After the chuck beef is browned, remove from the pan, and add another 1 tablespoon (15 ml) of oil if needed. Then add the green (smaller) leeks, shallots, garlic, and ginger. Lower the heat to medium-low, and season with salt, stirring occasionally, about 8–10 minutes, until softened. If there are bits burning on the bottom, add in a few spoonfuls of broth. Add the cinnamon, allspice, anise, and white pepper. Stir and cook for 1–2 minutes. Pour in the broth mixture and scrape the bottom, taste for salt.

(continued)

GOCHUJANG BABY BOK CHOY

2 tablespoons (108 g) gochujang chili paste

1 tablespoon (14 g) mayonnaise

1 tablespoon (15 ml) apple cider vinegar

1 tablespoon (15 ml) toasted sesame oil

1½ tablespoons (10 g) honey or (19 g) white sugar

salt to taste

2 tablespoons (30 ml) neutral oil

4–6 baby bok choy, halved

7. Finally, place the chuck roast into the center and surround it with the remaining white (larger) leeks and a pinch of salt. If you don't have a heavy lid, you'll need to secure a piece of foil on top to keep the liquids in.

8. Place on the center rack of the oven and bake for 2½–3 hours. After 30 minutes of braising, check to make sure the liquids are simmering; if not, increase the heat slightly. Midway through braising, carefully flip the meat and return to the oven. The meat is done when it is flaky, falling apart, and fork tender. Allow the meat to rest 15–30 minutes before serving.

TO MAKE THE BOK CHOY

9. While the meat rests, prepare the baby bok choy. In a small bowl, whisk together the gochujang, mayonnaise, apple cider vinegar, sesame oil, honey, and salt to taste. Heat 1 tablespoon (15 ml) of neutral oil over medium-high heat. Add a few teaspoons of gochujang sauce to the pan and place the bok choy cut side down. Season with salt and add 2 tablespoons (28 ml) of water. Cover and steam for 2–3 minutes until softened and caramelized on the bottom; you may need to lower the heat, remove the lid, and add a little more water until browned. Keep warm until ready to serve.

10. Serve with rice and blistered shishito peppers.

NOTES

- When cutting leeks, remove the dirty dried top layers, but keep the green parts. Chop the fibrous green ends into ½" (1 cm) pieces. When you get to the wider part, make the pieces larger, 2" (5 cm) thick.

- When choosing a braising dish, make sure it's small enough to keep the ingredients contained tightly. You want the liquids to condense right under the lid and the meat, ensuring it is constantly being basted, soaking up flavor. The liquids should cover about one-third of the ingredients. I recommend a shallow, medium-size heavy bottom skillet, a bistro baking braising dish, or a Dutch oven.

- Tip for blistering shishito peppers: In a skillet, heat neutral oil over medium-high heat. Add the peppers; sprinkle with kosher salt and cook for 4–5 minutes, turning semi-frequently to blister.

Chicken Mole Enchiladas

Saucy, smothered, cheesy enchiladas remind me of when my children were teens. Before they got home from sports practice, I would load and roll up tortillas with seasoned ground meat, cheese, and even sometimes sweet potato or other veggies, and douse them in bottled red enchilada sauce. When they came home, there would be a steaming dish of goodness waiting for them. My daughter developed this mole negro-inspired recipe as an ode to these delicious postpractice memories. Traditional Mexican moles come in many colors and textures, depending on the place of origin. Some recipes are relatively simple, and some take hours or even days. This recipe falls somewhere in the middle; it is a bit labor-intensive, but trust me, it pays off in the end.

Makes 5–6 cups (1.1–1.3 kg) mole | Serves 6–8 | Prep time: 25 minutes, plus 30-minute soak time | Cook time: 35 minutes

MOLE SAUCE

2 dried ancho chilis, stemmed and seeded

3 dried chili guajillo, stemmed and seeded

3 cloves garlic

¼ white onion

1 small tomato

½ cup (118 ml) vegetable oil or lard

⅓ cup (45 g) raw cashews, whole

½ cup (89) dates, roughly chopped

¼ cup (39 g) dried tart cherries

¼ cup (36 g) white sesame seeds

2 oz (6–7) Maria cookies (or graham crackers, or 1 cup [72 g] animal crackers) crushed

1 teaspoon black pepper

1½ (3.5 g) teaspoons ground cinnamon

2½ teaspoons whole coriander seeds, or 2 teaspoons ground coriander

3 tablespoons (48 g) peanut butter

1 tablespoon (20 g) honey or maple syrup, plus more to taste

2½ cups (570 ml) chicken stock

2 oz (55 g) dark Mexican chocolate, roughly chopped (or bittersweet Baker's chocolate)

salt to taste

MAKE THE MOLE

1. Bring 2½ cups (570 ml) of water to a boil. Set aside.

2. Heat a 12" (30 cm) skillet over high heat. Add the chilis in a single layer and toast on both sides, about 2 minutes. The chilis will become fragrant and softened. Transfer the chilis to a bowl and pour hot water over; let sit for 25–30 minutes until they have the consistency of wet leaves. Transfer chilis and 1½ cups (355 ml) soaking liquid into a blender and purée until smooth, set aside.

3. Heat the broiler to high. On a small baking sheet, add the garlic, white onion, and tomato. Broil, turning once, until charred, about 5 minutes for the garlic, 10 minutes for the tomato and onion; remove and set aside.

4. Heat ½ cup (118 ml) oil in a 12" (30 cm), high-walled skillet over medium-high heat. Make sure to have all your ingredients portioned out and ready to fry, as you don't want anything to burn. While frying, stir the ingredients constantly.

(continued)

ENCHILADAS

4–5 cups (448–580 g) shredded
  chicken

3½ cups (403 g) shredded Monterey
  Jack cheese, or mozzarella

8–10 8" (20 cm) flour tortillas

TO GARNISH

cilantro

pico de gallo

5. When the oil is hot, add the cashews, dates, and cherries, and fry for 90 seconds. Add the charred onion, garlic, tomato, then sesame seeds, and cookies, and fry for 90 more seconds. Finally, add the black pepper, cinnamon, coriander seeds, and peanut butter; fry for 90 seconds. Add the chili purée, honey, chicken stock, and chocolate. Bring to a boil, then reduce the heat to medium-low and simmer for 3–4 minutes. Remove from the heat and transfer to a blender; purée until very smooth. Taste for additional salt and honey; set aside.

ASSEMBLE ENCHILADAS

6. Preheat the oven to 400°F (200°C, or gas mark 6) and grease a 9" x 13" (23 x 33 cm) baking dish.

7. Spread about 1 cup of mole (224 g) on the bottom of the pan. Divide the chicken and about 1½ cups (173 g) of cheese into the tortillas; roll up and arrange tightly in the pan. Cover with about 2 more cups (475 ml) of sauce, spreading into any gaps, and top with the remaining cheese.

8. Bake for 20–24 minutes, or until the sauce is bubbling around the edges and the cheese is golden. Serve with cilantro and pico de gallo.

NOTES

- For the shredded chicken, I prefer to use rotisserie to save time.
- You can substitute store-bought sauce for the homemade variety.

Toasted Milk Cheesecake with Corn Flake Crust

Milk solids are the tiny, browned granules you see at the bottom of browned butter—they're caramelly, nutty, and compliment both sweet and savory flavors. This recipe uses toasted milk solids to give the batter a subtle roasted flavor, a bit more complex than a classic cheesecake. The toasted corn flake crust, too, has caramel qualities that perfectly complement the cake.

Serves 8–10 | Prep time: 10 minutes | Cook time: 65–75 minutes, plus 6-hour cooling time

CRUST

5½ cups (176 g) corn flakes

10 tablespoons (253 g) butter, divided

⅓ cup (75 g) and 1 tablespoon (15 g) brown sugar

¾ teaspoon kosher salt

FILLING

¼ cup (32 g) milk solids (milk powder)

24 oz (680 g) cream cheese, softened at room temperature

1⅓ cups (267 g) white sugar

4 eggs, 2 yolks, room temperature

½ cup (115 g) full-fat sour cream, room temperature

1½ teaspoons kosher salt

1 tablespoon (15 ml) vanilla extract

1. Preheat the oven to 300°F (150°C, or gas mark 2) and grease the bottom of a 9–10" (23–25 cm) springform pan.

2. In a small skillet over medium heat, add the milk solids. Using a whisk, stir and toast until golden and fragrant; 4–5 minutes. Set aside.

3. On a sheet pan, spread the corn flakes into a single layer. Melt 4 tablespoons (55 g) of butter and drizzle over the corn flakes, tossing to coat with your hands. Bake for 12–15 minutes until darkened and fragrant. Set aside and let cool for 3–5 minutes.

4. In a food processor, add the corn flakes and pulse until fine and sandlike. Melt the remaining 6 tablespoons (85 g) of butter and add to the cornflakes along with the brown sugar and salt. Pulse until fine and can hold together when pressed in the palm of your hand. Press the crust into the springform pan using the bottom of a measuring cup, going up the sides ½–¾" (1–2 cm). Bake at 300°F (150°C, or gas mark 2) for 8 minutes. Remove from the oven and let cool completely. Once cooled, grease the sides with melted butter and wrap the pan thoroughly in foil, double-wrapped if needed, so that no water leaks into the cake. Place in a high-walled baking dish and set aside.

5. Preheat the oven to 325°F (170°C, or gas mark 3).

(continued)

6. Make the filling: In a stand mixer, or using a hand mixer, beat together the cream cheese and sugar on medium speed until silky. Scrape down the sides and bottom of the bowl, then add the eggs and yolks, mix at medium speed and wait at least 30 seconds in between each addition. Scrape down the sides and bottom of the bowl very well, then mix in the sour cream. Finally, add the salt, vanilla, and sifted, toasted milk solids. Mix on medium-low until creamy.

7. Boil 1–2 quarts (946 ml–1.9 L) of water. Pour the cheesecake filling onto the cooled crust and gently tap the pan on the counter.

8. Transfer to the center rack of the oven and bake for 60–70 minutes; the edges should be firm, and the center should have a slight jiggle. Once removed from the oven and cooled for at least 1 hour, use a knife to separate the edge of the cake from the pan, leaving the cake in the pan to chill. Refrigerate the cake for at least 6 hours, preferably overnight, before serving.

9. Serve with creamy Creamy Vanilla Lemon Curd (page 91) and/or fresh fruit.

NOTES

- It's important to not mix ingredients at high speeds, to avoid bubbles in the batter.
- If you can't find milk solids (milk powder), simply omit it *or* add another flavor like lemon, by incorporating 3 tablespoons (18 g) citrus zest into the batter.
- You can swap out the crust for a more traditional graham cracker version if you prefer.
- It is essential that all ingredients be at room temperature. If you're in a pinch, use your microwave on 20 percent power and heat individual ingredients in 15–30-second intervals until they reach room temperature.
- Make sure to *religiously* scrape down the sides and bottom of the bowl after each ingredient incorporation to ensure there isn't a thick, chunky layer at the bottom when the batter is poured out.
- When baking in the water bath, very securely wrap the springform pan in foil, two to three layers if needed. If you're unsure of how to prepare a water bath, watch an online video for clarification.
- If the top splits or browns, who really cares? A cheesecake is a cheesecake, and we don't have time for perfection here!

Baked Brie Dinner Board

A cheese board for dinner? Yes, please! This board is my solution to this cheesy dinner dream; guests add whatever they want to their Brie ramekin, and bake it into a savory and sweet oozing, bubbly meal, complete with crunchy crackers and fresh fruits and greens to add postbake. Cheers for eating cheese for dinner!

Serves 6 | Prep time: 30 minutes | Cook time: 25 minutes | Made on the 26" (66 cm) Big Board

2 x 14 oz (400 g) brie rounds, cubed into 1" (2.5 cm) pieces

1 lb. (455 g) spicy Italian sausage, cooked

8 oz (225 g) pancetta, cooked

2 cups (140 g) sautéed mushrooms or another plant-based meat alternative

⅓ cup (100 g) onion jam

⅓ cup (100 g) blackberry jam

⅓ cup (87 g) pesto

¼ cup (14 g) sun-dried tomatoes

fresh tomatoes

1 heaping cup (170 g) pitted dates

6 servings crackers

2 oz (55 g) prosciutto

2 oz (55 g) Calabrese salami

1 Epi baguette

1 cup (100 g) toasted pecans

½ cup (72.5 g) rosemary Marcona almonds

⅓ cup (45 g) roasted hazelnuts

1 Bartlett pear, sliced

3 apples, sliced (Opal, Granny Smith, and Honeycrisp)

3 cup (90 g) arugula or other tender green, like spinach

1 cup (150 g) cherry tomatoes, sliced

wine to serve

1. Preheat the oven to 400°F (200°C, or gas mark 6).

2. Divide the cheese cubes into single-serving ramekins.

3. Place the meats, mushrooms, jams, spreads, sun-dried tomatoes, and fresh tomatoes into bowls; arrange the bowls on the board first, then fill in with the remaining ingredients.

4. To assemble the ramekins, have guests add up to ½ cup (115 g) of toppings and mix-ins to their ramekins. Add fresh ingredients like fruit, greens, and tomatoes, to serve with the Brie after it is baked in each ramekin. TIP: To keep track of whose dish is whose, arrange the ramekins on a baking sheet lined with parchment; mark initials next to each ramekin.

5. Bake the cheese until bubbling; 20–25 minutes.

6. Serve each individual brie bowl with the remaining fresh fruits, veggies, crackers, breads, and nuts.

NOTES

- Add 2 cups (140 g) of a meat alternative, like sautéed mushrooms or spiced plant-based meat for a vegetarian option.

- Toss the fresh fruits in a bit of lemon juice to prevent browning.

Tea Affogato

Classic affogato, or "affogato al caffe," drowns vanilla ice cream in hot, bitter espresso, melting into a dreamy, drinkable dessert. The same can be done with tea—and not just Earl Grey, but Chai and green tea as well. You can also mix up the ice cream flavors; classic vanilla is my go-to, but other options that would pair well with herbaceous or spiced teas are lemon, green tea, lavender, honey, and even pistachio. This is a great, two-ingredient dessert that requires little to no effort and will make you feel like you're sitting in a Florentine cafe. I recommend you let the tea cool off just a little before you splash in your ice cream. Additionally, make sure the tea is fresh and strongly brewed for maximum flavor.

Serves 4–6 | Prep time: 5 minutes

4–6 servings vanilla ice cream

4–6 servings strongly brewed Earl Grey tea

1. Portion out the ice cream into bowls. Once the tea has brewed and cooled a few minutes, drown each scoop in the hot tea and serve immediately.

CHAPTER 6

Go Explore: Recipes for the Great Outdoors

Deli Sandwich Takeout Board with Garden Salad

Takeout is an entertainer's gift from above! I never mind taking a culinary shortcut to prioritize community—and maximize my time outside! The more stress-free the gathering, the better.

For a quick outdoor board, I order the main dish—be it sandwiches, burgers, or pizza—and make up a quick side dish, like a garden salad with dressing. You can ask whoever you're meeting up with to bring a sweet treat and a side as well.

Serves 4–6 | Prep time: 15 minutes | Made on the 26" (66 cm) Big Board

DELI SANDWICHES

4–6 sandwiches

3 cups (93.8 g) kettle chips

4–6 servings dessert of choice

2 oranges, sliced

1 bunch grapes

CRUNCHY GARDEN SALAD

4 cups (220 g) spring mix or other lettuce

¾ cup (112.5 g) cherry tomatoes, halved

1 large Persian cucumber, sliced

2 large stalks celery, finely sliced or peeled

1 small apple, or other seasonal fruit, sliced

1½ cups (225 g) baby bell peppers, thinly sliced

¾ cup (67 g) jicama, julienned or shaven

⅓ cup (80 ml) dressing to serve

NOTE

- A garden salad is always a safe bet for me. Normally I would put nuts on a salad, but the veggies here are *so* crunchy that it isn't necessary. You can swap out any of the veggies and fruit for what's in season.

Hiking Lamb Harissa Chili Board

One of my favorite things about living in Oregon is that we get to experience all the seasons (sometimes in a single day). By the end of summer, I'm waiting (impatiently) for the day that grocery stores begin to carry my favorite fall produce. The chilis I grew up eating consisted of basic tomatoes, beef, onions, beans, and a variety of Tex-Mex condiments, like shredded cheese, sour cream, tortilla chips, and lime. I still love them, because they taste like home, but sometimes the familiar is just too . . . familiar. So I developed this Lamb Harissa Chili, desiring the familiarly unfamiliar. Aside from the poblano chilis, the spices, flavors, techniques, and ingredients are influenced by Mediterranean and North African cuisines. My favorite part of this chili is the addition of Baba Ghanoush (page 20) because it lends a creamy, nutty flavor to the final product.

Serves 4–6 | Made on the 12" x 24" (30 x 60 cm) Travel Board

LAMB HARISSA CHILI

1 lb. (455 g) ground lamb

2 teaspoons kosher salt, plus more to taste

2 teaspoons fresh black pepper

1 teaspoon ground cinnamon

2½ teaspoons ground cumin

1½ teaspoons sweet paprika

2 tablespoons (30 ml) olive oil

7–8 baby bell peppers, cut into ¼" (6 mm) strips (or diced)

1 yellow onion, diced

5–6 cloves garlic, crushed

7 dates, roughly chopped

1 tablespoon (15 g) harissa paste, plus 1 tablespoon (15 g) for extra spice

1 teaspoon sumac

2 x 14-oz (400 g) cans fire roasted tomatoes

1 x 14-oz (400 g) can chickpeas, drained

3 cups (705 ml) vegetable or chicken broth

1 recipe Baba Ghanoush (page 20)

1. In a shallow bowl, spread the lamb into a thin layer. Sprinkle with kosher salt, black pepper, cinnamon, cumin, and paprika. Gently mix with your hands or a spatula; set aside.

2. In a large, shallow braiser or wide baking dish, add the olive oil and heat over medium-high. Once shimmery, add the seasoned lamb. Let sit undisturbed for 2 minutes or so. Once the bottom has browned, break apart into smaller pieces and continue cooking 4–5 minutes more. When the lamb is cooked, remove the pot from the heat and use a slotted spoon to transfer the meat to a bowl, leaving behind the rendered fat.

3. Turn the heat back to medium-high and add the bell peppers, onion, garlic, dates, harissa paste, and salt to taste. Cook, stirring semi-frequently, for about 90 seconds, then reduce the heat to medium-low and add the sumac. Cook until the peppers and onions are softened, 8–9 minutes.

4. Stir in the tomatoes, chickpeas, and broth. Bring to a simmer, stir in the Baba Ghanoush, and reduce for 8–10 minutes. Stir in the lamb, taste for salt, and simmer for 18–22 minutes more until thickened. Taste for additional spices and salt.

FOR THE BOARD

4 pitas, quartered

½ cup (75 g) crumbled feta cheese

⅔ cup (120 g) Kalamata olives

2 baby bell peppers, julienned

¼ cup (15 g) chopped mint

¼ cup (15 g) chopped parsley

1–2 navel oranges, sliced

4 stroopwafels or other cookies

chai packets

5. Serve with toasted pita, or other flat bread, crumbled feta cheese, Kalamata olives, extra lemon juice, fresh bell pepper for crunch, mint, parsley, and a side of fruit. For a sweet bite, stroopwafel and warm chai is our go-to!

NOTE

- Take your time when making this fall-time favorite. This recipe is great to take on an evening hike. We used a portable propane stove to reheat it, but it can be eaten cold too. For a sweet bite afterward, stroopwafels and hot tea are a great combination, but cookies, granola bars, or a chocolaty trail mix are great options too.

Après-ski Seafood Potpie Soup Board

Potpies are definitely one of my top three comfort foods, and certainly what I crave after a cold day spent in the outdoors. Unfortunately, they don't travel well, especially when you're on top of a cold mountain without access to an oven! My solution: a deconstructed potpie soup. The Hot Buttered Rum Mix, puff pastry pinwheels, and base of this creamy, decadent potpie soup can be made ahead of time, which makes preparation and traveling a breeze—just prepare your board with your desired fixings, bring the base to a simmer on a camp stove, then add the seafood 10 minutes or so before you're ready to feast.

Serve on the 26" (66 cm) Big Board

FOR THE BOARD

one pot of Seafood Potpie Soup
(page 204)

one batch pinwheels (the recipe uses
2 sheets puff pastry)

Spanish Tortas de Aceite (sweet anise
tortas)

pistachios

mixed seasoned nuts

Parmesan cheese

finely chopped parsley

grapes, apple, blood orange, cherries

mini lemon tea cake cookies

chocolate biscotti

8 bottles of rum/whiskey/bourbon

1 jar of Hot Buttered Rum recipe
(page 205)

NOTES

- If you don't want to make the pinwheels, warm, sliced baguette on the side works just as well.

- To make this ahead of time, make the broth without adding the seafood. Then, about 20 minutes before serving, bring the broth to a simmer, add the seafood, and cook for 8–10 minutes; serve immediately.

- This can be made with a single, cheaper type of protein if needed—a firm, white flesh fish like mahi mahi or even salmon would work as well.

- Fill Mason jars with the hot buttered rum mix for holiday gifts! It can also be frozen for later: Once refrigerated and hard, wrap the butter in wax paper and roll into small logs, seal by twisting the ends, and place in plastic wrap to freeze. Remove from the freezer, slice into small pieces, and place in a mug with boiling water.

Seafood Potpie Soup

Serves 6–8 | Prep time: 30 minutes | Cook time: 60–90 minutes

8 oz (225 g) pancetta, diced

5 tablespoons (64 g) butter

1 large yellow onion, medium diced

1 cup (130 g) carrot, peeled, medium diced

1 large bulb fennel, finely diced

4 cups (280 g) cremini mushrooms, roughly chopped

pinch of salt

fresh black pepper

¼ cup (31 g) all-purpose flour

3 tablespoons (45 ml) fish sauce

1 tablespoon (15 ml) soy sauce

42 oz (3 x 14-oz [425 ml] cans) seafood stock

2 cups (260 g) frozen peas

1 lb. (455 g) large shrimp, peeled, deveined and halved

1 lb. (455 g) large dry scallops, halved

½ lb. (225 g) fresh crab meat

⅓ cup (80 ml) heavy cream

⅓ cup (20 g) parsley, minced

1. In a cold, heavy bottom pot, add the pancetta, and bring the heat to medium-low. Render the fat, about 6 minutes. Use a slotted spoon to remove the pancetta, then add the butter.

2. Melt the butter over medium-low heat; add the onions, carrots, fennel, mushrooms, a pinch of salt, and a few cracks of pepper. Cook for 15 minutes, until the vegetables are softened.

3. Lower the heat to medium-low and add the flour, mixing in until incorporated, then add back in the pancetta and rendered fat—cook 3–4 minutes.

4. Add the fish sauce and soy sauce to the pan to deglaze; scrape the bottom of the pan and cook for 1 minute, then add the seafood stock. Bring to a boil, then add the peas and reduce to a simmer, 10 minutes.

5. Add the seafood to the soup along with the heavy cream. Simmer for 10–12 minutes, or until the seafood is opaque and just cooked. Garnish with parsley and serve immediately. Optional to serve with the pinwheels, adding one to the bottom of the bowl before serving the soup, and one on top. Or just dip them into the broth of the soup.

Puff Pastry Pinwheels

Makes 32 bites | Prep time: 15 minutes | Cook time: 18–20 minutes

2 sheets puff pastry, thawed

½ cup (160 g) caramelized onions or onion jam, divided (optional)

⅔ cup (76 g) shredded sharp cheddar cheese, divided

¾ cup (60 g) crumbled Parmesan

1 egg, beaten with 1 teaspoon water

1. Preheat the oven to 400°F (200°C, or gas mark 6) and line two baking sheets with parchment paper.

2. Roll out the puff pastry into a 10" x 11" (25 x 28 cm) rectangle. Divide the onions onto each sheet and spread into a single layer. Sprinkle half of the sharp cheddar and Parmesan cheese onto each sheet in a single layer. Roll up each sheet, and using a serrated knife, divide each log into sixteen wheels.

3. Arrange the wheels on the tray about ½" (1 cm) apart. Brush on the beaten egg wash, then bake for 18–20 minutes until golden on top. Be careful not to bake the wheels too long, as the sugar from the onions will burn.

Hot Buttered Rum

Serves 12 | Prep time: 5 minutes | Makes about 2 cups (475 ml)

1 cup (2 sticks [225 g]) unsalted butter, softened

1 teaspoon vanilla extract

¾ cup (170 g) dark brown sugar

2 teaspoons ground cinnamon

2¼ teaspoons cardamom

½ teaspoon fresh ground nutmeg

¼ teaspoon ground cloves

pinch of salt

dark rum to serve

1. In a stand mixer, cream together the butter, vanilla, sugar, spices, and salt, until the sugar is mostly dissolved and the color is a light brown, about 5 minutes.

2. Pack into small glass jars and store in the refrigerator.

3. Add 2 tablespoons (28 g) of the butter into a mug and add 6 ounces (175 ml) hot water; stir until dissolved, then add 2 ounces (60 ml) of rum into the mug.

4. Serve hot with sweet treats for dipping.

Warming Hut Brothy Quinoa Bowls Board

A wind-chilled hike to Swampy Lake warming shelter in Bend, Oregon, calls for two things: a roaring fire and a comforting, nutritious meal. Instant quinoa bowls are lightweight, healthy, and simple to serve. Add as many chopped veggies and beans as you like—tomatoes and olives add a much-needed acidic touch—and make sure you don't skip the bouillon or Parmesan, as they're the flavor-packed secret weapons. For dessert, bring mugs and instant coffee to enjoy with cookies and chocolates.

Bring wooden or other lightweight bowls to assemble the board. The cook time will vary depending on the brand of instant quinoa or other grain. We use instant quinoa that takes about 3 minutes to absorb the broth. I recommend having a portable stove to heat the water or bring a pot and utilize the stove in the warming hut. Bring foil to cover the pot, or individual bowls to allow the grains to cook fully. If desired, add the kale to wilt it.

Serves 4–6 | Prep time: 15 minutes | Cook time: 3–10 minutes (varies) | Serve on a 20" (51 cm) board

---

4 servings instant quinoa, or other instant grain

4 servings vegetable bouillon cubes

1 x 14-oz (240 g) can chickpeas, drained

1 cup (150 g) cherry tomatoes, halved

⅔ cup (67 g) sliced pitted green olives

⅓ cup (27 g) shredded Parmesan cheese

3 cups (201 g) Tuscan kale, finely chopped

8–10 baguette slices

1 Opal apple, sliced, tossed in lemon juice (optional)

1–2 Cara Cara oranges, sliced

4 servings of dessert of your choice (bites)

coffee for serving

1. To make the bowls, cook the instant grains according to the package directions with vegetable bouillon, adding extra water and bouillon for a brothier meal.

2. Assemble the board while the grains cook; arrange the chickpeas, tomatoes, olives, cheese, and bouillon cubes into bowls. On the board arrange the kale, bread, fruit, and desserts.

Hot Chocolate Firepit Board with Buttermilk Rough Puff Pastry Ribbons

These buttermilk ribbons are one of my favorite desserts in this book. A warning—if left on the countertop after baking, they will be gone in a matter of minutes! They're flaky, a little tangy, and have a crunchy coat of cinnamon sugar on the outside. They can be stored uncovered at room temperature, and the dough will be moist and buttery. Dip them in hot chocolate, whipped cream, sweet spreads, or just eat them by themselves.

Made on the 20" (51 cm) Big Board

8 servings Cinnamon Vanilla Hot Chocolate

2 cups (120 g) Tangy Whipped Cream (page 90)

⅓ cup (86 g) chocolate hazelnut spread

2 dozen Buttermilk Rough Puff Pastry Ribbons

4 oz (115 g) mini shortbread cookies

12 chocolate-covered cherries

12 candy canes

6 oz (170 g) toffee milk chocolate-covered crackers

5 oz (140 g) mini marshmallows

6 oz (170 g) peppermint bark

5 oz (140 g) salted caramel-flavored meringue cookies

NOTES

- The pastry can be made 3 days in advance.

- I recommend grating the butter cube when it's frozen, then returning to the freezer for a few minutes to rechill.

- For the cinnamon, brown sugar coat, make sure the softened butter can be spread out with a pastry brush; if needed, heat in the microwave at 10 percent power, in 5–10-second intervals, just until spreadable.

- As with any pastry dough, handle it as little as possible for a tender result. Additionally, make sure the butter doesn't soften or melt while handling it; this will result in a flat dough that leaks butter.

- Spice up hot cocoa with: cinnamon, vanilla, dark chocolate, a pinch of chili powder for a kick, a pinch of salt, or serve with mini bottles of Bailey's Irish Cream for an adult-friendly outdoor gathering!

Buttermilk Rough Puff Pastry Ribbons

Makes 12 ribbons | Prep time: 15 minutes, plus 30-minute chill time and 30-minute rest time |
Cook time: 20 minutes, plus 10-minute cool time

PUFF PASTRY

1½ cups (187.5 g) all-purpose flour

½ heaping teaspoon kosher salt

1¼ teaspoons white sugar

¾ cup (12 tablespoons) (170 g) unsalted butter, grated, frozen

⅓–½ cup (80–120 ml) buttermilk, in ice

SPICED SUGAR

3 tablespoons (12 g) white sugar

2 tablespoons (30 g) brown sugar

1 teaspoon ground cinnamon

pinch of allspice

¼ heaping teaspoon salt

4 tablespoons (55 g) butter, softened

1. In a shallow mixing bowl, mix the flour, salt, and sugar. Add in all the butter and toss with your hands to coat in flour. Create a well in the center and pour in about 3 tablespoons (45 ml) of the chilled buttermilk. Using your hands, lift the flour in an upward motion until the buttermilk is dispersed. Repeat this step, adding 1–2 tablespoons (15–30 ml) of buttermilk at a time, until the dough begins to come together and just holds its shape when squeezed in your palm, like damp sand. Try not to over-hydrate the dough.

2. When the dough holds together, begin folding it on top of itself until a disk is just formed. The dough will have a few cracks, however, if it is tacky to the touch and a little over-hydrated. Simply use a little extra flour when rolling it out to compensate.

3. Shape the disk into a rectangle and transfer to a sheet of plastic wrap; cover tightly and refrigerate for at least 30 minutes to further hydrate. This can also be done overnight; just slow the dough to rest at room temperature for 30 minutes before rolling out.

4. While the dough chills, combine the white sugar, brown sugar, cinnamon, allspice, and salt in a small bowl. Set aside.

5. Preheat the oven to 350°F (180°C, or gas mark 4) and line a large baking sheet with parchment.

6. Roughly roll out the dough into a 13" x 9" (33 x 23 cm) rectangle. Trim the sides so they're straight; it should trim down to a 12" x 8" (30 x 20 cm) rectangle. Using a pastry brush, spread the softened butter all over, and sprinkle with about half of the cinnamon sugar. Flip the dough and repeat, so both sides are coated. Using a ruler and a knife, mark 12 1" (2.5 cm) segments across the top. Cut the dough into long strips using a knife and a straight edge. Twist the strips into spirals and place on the sheet tray about 1" (2.5 cm) apart.

7. Place on the center rack of the oven and bake for 20–22 minutes, until the ribbons are puffed and golden on the bottom. While in the oven, the butter and sugar on the outside will caramelize deliciously into a crunchy coating but be careful to not overbake and burn the sugar.

8. Once baked, remove from the oven and set to cool on a rack for at least 10 minutes.

Cinnamon Vanilla Hot Chocolate

Makes about 8½ cup (120 ml) servings | Prep time: 5 minutes | Cook time: 10 minutes

3 tablespoons (16 g) cocoa powder

1 teaspoon ground cinnamon

⅔ cup (134 g) white sugar

pinch of salt

4½ cups (1.07 L) whole milk

2 teaspoons vanilla extract

3 oz (85 g) 60 percent bakers' chocolate, finely chopped

1. In a medium sauce pot, whisk together the cocoa powder, cinnamon, sugar, and salt. Add the milk and bring the mixture to a boil, then reduce to a simmer. Whisk until the sugar is dissolved, then remove from the heat, and add the vanilla and chocolate. Stir until the chocolate melts and the hot cocoa is creamy. Keep warm until ready to serve.

ACKNOWLEDGMENTS

This outdoorsy cookbook has been a fun one! I'm so thankful for the whole team involved, from the initial concept (let's take the board outside) to the last design. Thank you!

To the Big Board and Reluctant Entertainer communities, this book is for you! Thank you for sharing the same passion for hosting, for making my recipes, and sharing them with your friends and family.

Abby, I can't even begin to thank you for all the work you did to make this book happen. You are my beautiful daughter and friend—so talented with your recipes, food styling, photography, and ideas. Oh, and then traveling, eating, planning, and creating. Up at 4:45 a.m. for the sunrise, the perfect spot in Napa Valley, the windy day on the California beach. The most fun—Dad and me sharing the airstream with you. :)

To Chris, Carma, Patti, Kim, Brian and Lori, Elliot, Paul, and Abby—for the outdoor adventures—hiking in the snow, tailgating at Mt. Bachelor, and climbing to the top of Smith Rock. Eating on The Big Board was the icing on the cake. Meg and Gary, for a chilly dinner on Cardinal Landing with the best ever sandwiches. And then again, to Elliot, Chris, and Abby, for carrying me off (and back up again) the mountain (another story for another day).

Cyndi, you came along at the perfect time to help launch The Big Board and include me in your House of Hyacinth store. It's been a fun journey, and WOW! J.K. Adams lives up to their reputation of being the best wood makers in the United States!

To Adrienne, for being my #1 recipe tester and special childhood friend. Even up to the last minute you were testing, testing, testing. The hours you put into this book will never be forgotten. And to Carma, Patti, Cindy and Tom, Marie, Laurel, Sarah, and Ginny—a big, big thank you for your valuable recipe input.

To Barb—always helping me with edits, with so much love and support for our family, and who has believed in RE from the beginning.

Thank you to my agent Cyle Young and to the amazing team at Quarto: Emily, Liz, Erik, David, Jeff, and Todd; I love working with you all.

Grace, for the little things—here and there. Always willing to help.

Paul and Elliot—for the quick few months of tasting and helping out, and to Elliot—carrying that board up to the top of Smith Rock! Thank you to Garrett and Vicky, now home in the States, and to Elliot, Abby, and Paul for your constant love and support.

And now—*Feast on Life*!

ABOUT THE AUTHOR

Sandy Coughlin is the delightful cheerleader and guru of all things related to food, travel, "big board" dinner and charcuterie ideas, and hospitality on her blog, *Reluctant Entertainer*. Her love is to help readers and reluctant entertainers with easy tips, tasty recipes, and inspiration so they, too, can open their hearts and homes to beloved guests.

Coughlin is the author of *Big Boards for Families* (2021), and *The Reluctant Entertainer* (2010). She has been featured by *Taste of Home*, EatingWell, *Better Homes and Gardens*, *New York Post*, and ThePioneerWoman.com. She is a mother to three grown children and one adorable daughter-in-law and lives in Bend, Oregon, with her husband Paul. You can find her on social media @ReluctantEntertainer.

ABOUT THE PHOTOGRAPHER

Abby Coughlin is a photographer living in the San Francisco Bay Area. After nearly 10 years of practicing photography as a hobby, she decided to pursue it professionally after graduating from college with a degree in music. In addition to photography, she is a budding food stylist and recipe developer, having photographed, styled, and developed recipes for *Big Boards for Families* cookbook. To her, there are a few things more joy-inducing than preparing a meal and sharing it with loved ones.

INDEX